the drawings of / les dessins de
Norman McLaren

"Film making is my work. Drawing is my play."

"Je réalise des films par profession; je dessine par plaisir."

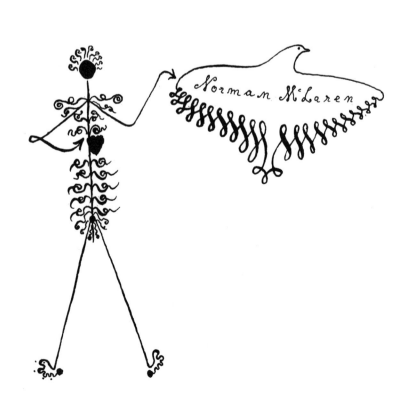

the drawings of / les dessins de
Norman McLaren

Text by Norman McLaren
edited from taped interviews by Michael White

Commentaires de Norman McLaren
rédigés par Michael White d'après des interviews enregistrées

Tundra Books  Les Livres Toundra

©1975, Norman McLaren

Tundra Books of Montreal
Montreal, Quebec H3G 1J6

ISBN 0-88776-161-9
Legal Deposit, Third Quarter
Quebec National Library

Published simultaneously in the United States by
Tundra Books of Northern New York
Plattsburgh, New York 12901

Library of Congress Card No. 75-17133
ISBN 0-912766-28-X

Edited by Michael White

French translation by René Chicoine

Design concept by Booze & Delaney
Design and production by Molly Pulver, Montreal

Typeset by Compoplus, Montreal, in 11 on 13 point Goudy
Printed in the United States by Froelich/Greene Inc.
Bound by A. Horowitz & Son

Tundra Books Inc. has applied funds from its Canada Council
block grant for 1975 towards the editing and production of
this book.

Michael White also wishes to acknowledge the assistance given
him by the Canada Council during the compilation of this book.

©1975, Norman McLaren

Les Livres Toundra de Montréal
Montréal, Québec H3G 1J6

ISBN 0-88776-161-9
Dépôt légal, 3ᵉ trimestre
Bibliothèque nationale du Québec

Publiée simultanément aux États-Unis, par
Tundra Books of Northern New York
Plattsburgh, New York 12901

Fiche de la Library of Congress no 75-17133
ISBN 0-912766-28-X

Compilation: Michael White

Traduction française: René Chicoine

Maquette: Booze & Delaney
Disposition bilingue: Molly Pulver, Montréal

Typographie: Compoplus, Montréal - Caractères Goudy,
corps 11
Imprimé aux États-Unis par Froelich/Greene Inc.
Relié par A. Horowitz & Son

Pour la compilation et l'édition du présent volume, les Livres
Toundra (Inc.) ont puisé à la subvention globale que le Conseil
des Arts leur a accordée pour l'année 1975.

Michael White désire, pour sa part, remercier le Conseil des
Arts pour lui avoir facilité la compilation de l'ouvrage.

Table
of contents

Table
des matières

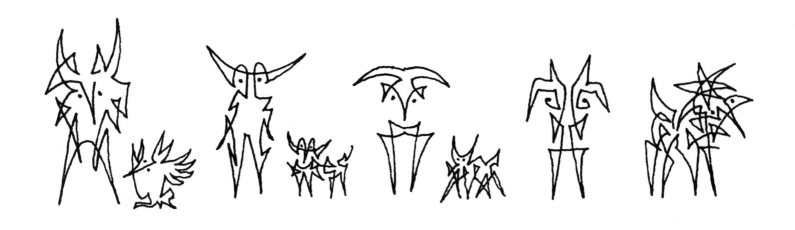

Film making is my work, and my kind of film making has often involved drawing — of a laborious and specialized kind. The drawings in this collection, done over quite a long period, are the product of my love of drawing just for its own sake. When free of the demands of film making, and when relaxed, I have found in pen and ink a kind of serious play.

Such drawings being technically simple, direct and usually improvised lent themselves to a fairly rapid execution of ideas arising often from my subconscious mind. If they succeeded — good; if they failed — no matter . . . I could always try something else.

Thus the drawings were done mostly for myself with no particular "public" in mind — again in marked contrast to my film work.

What I feel when creating is more than mere pleasure; I am fulfilling a need as important (and, if I'm lucky, as natural) as breathing.

Montreal, 14 July 1975

Cinéaste par profession, j'utilise souvent le dessin — un dessin absorbant et spécialisé. Les études réunies ici, nés de mon amour du dessin pour le dessin, couvrent une période assez étendue. Quand mon occupation me laisse un peu de répit et que je me sens détendu, je trouve matière à un jeu sérieux dans l'utilisation de la plume et de l'encre.

Ce genre de dessins, de facture simple et généralement improvisés, permettent l'exécution relativement rapide de motifs qui souvent surgissent du subconscient. Si c'était réussi, tant mieux; si c'était raté, peu importe . . . Je pouvais toujours tenter autre chose.

C'est ainsi que ces dessins, je les ai faits surtout pour moi-même, et sans penser à un "public" en particulier — ce qui établit un fort contraste avec mon travail sur pellicule.

La création est plus qu'un plaisir pour moi; elle satisfait un besoin aussi vital que la respiration (et aussi naturel quand la chance me sourit).

Montréal, 14 juillet 1975

Norman McLaren

At art school in Glasgow we always worked from life or plaster casts. I came to hate drawing. The emphasis was on meticulous rendering of static poses lasting days and weeks. It was painstaking and boring and I was no good at it. However, just at that time I was discovering the cinema. I felt film was the art of the future. I neglected my art school classes and made movies instead. I failed my diploma but that in no way perturbed me. For two years after art school I dropped all graphic work. Then I discovered surrealism. It was liberating and exhilarating. I started to paint and draw again eagerly.

I kept very few drawings from art school and New York. My earliest pen and inks show the influence of surrealism, but do not all depict an "inner" world. The furniture designs were a protest against the rigid and angular style of the period. There are references to Ottawa, where I lived, Auschwitz and the war.

À l'école d'art de Glasgow, nous travaillions toujours d'après les plâtres et le modèle vivant. J'en vins à détester le dessin. On exigeait le rendu méticuleux de poses statiques qui duraient des jours et des semaines. C'était laborieux et assommant, d'autant plus que j'étais médiocre. À l'époque, cependant, je découvrais le cinéma et le pressentais comme l'art de l'avenir. Je me mis à en faire au détriment de mes études d'art et fus refusé au diplôme, ce qui me laissa indifférent. Deux années après mes études, j'abandonnai tout genre de travail graphique. Puis je découvris le surréalisme, que je trouvai vivifiant et libérateur. De nouveau je me remis allègrement au dessin et à la peinture.

J'ai conservé très peu de dessins du temps de mes études d'art et de mon séjour à New York. Mes tout premiers dessins à la plume trahissent une influence surréaliste, mais ne décrivent pas tous un monde intérieur. Avec les modèles de meubles, j'ai voulu protester contre le style anguleux et rigide de l'époque. Quelques-autres dessins se rapportent à Ottawa, où j'ai vécu, ainsi qu'à Auschwitz et à la guerre.

Sketch for a summer house   1944   pencil
The fanciful skyline of the Parliament Buildings in Ottawa delighted me.

Croquis d'un pavillon à la campagne   1944   mine de plomb
Je trouvais amusante la silhouette plutôt imprévue des édifices du Parlement.

1

Early
drawings

Les premiers
dessins

untitled   1948   pencil

sans titre   1948   mine de plomb

Love chair for two

Chair for One or Two
(Sex if two, masturbation if one)
May 1944

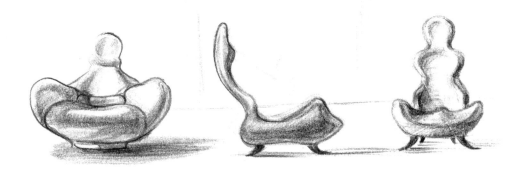

Anatomical Ordinary sitting chair

May 1944

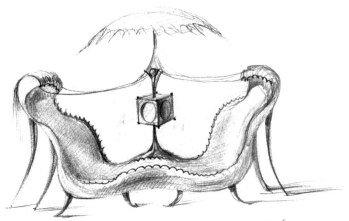

A Face to face Double chair
with built in small television screens.
for a summer garden

May 1944

Love-seat for two

Sketches for furniture of the future 1944 pencil
I felt the furniture of the thirties drab and formal.

Croquis d'ameublement futuriste 1944 mine de plomb
L'ameublement, dans les années 30, me semblait terne et pompeux.

"After the war!"
Sketch for women's clothes   1944   quill pen and pencil
During the war, women's clothes were very dull. The swings of fashion had always intrigued me, so I took a shot at imagining what they would be like twenty to thirty years hence.

Après la guerre
Esquisse de vêtements féminins   1944   plume d'oie et mine de plomb
Le vêtement féminin, pendant la guerre, n'offrait aucun intérêt. L'évolution de la mode m'ayant toujours intrigué, je m'essayai à imaginer quelle forme elle prendrait vingt ou trente ans plus tard.

Interlocking faces 1944 quill pen and india ink
If I remember rightly, I had recently visited a very small,
crowded sauna.

Enclenchement 1944 plume d'oie et encre de
Chine
Si je me souviens bien, j'avais visité, il y avait peu, un
sauna bondé et exigu.

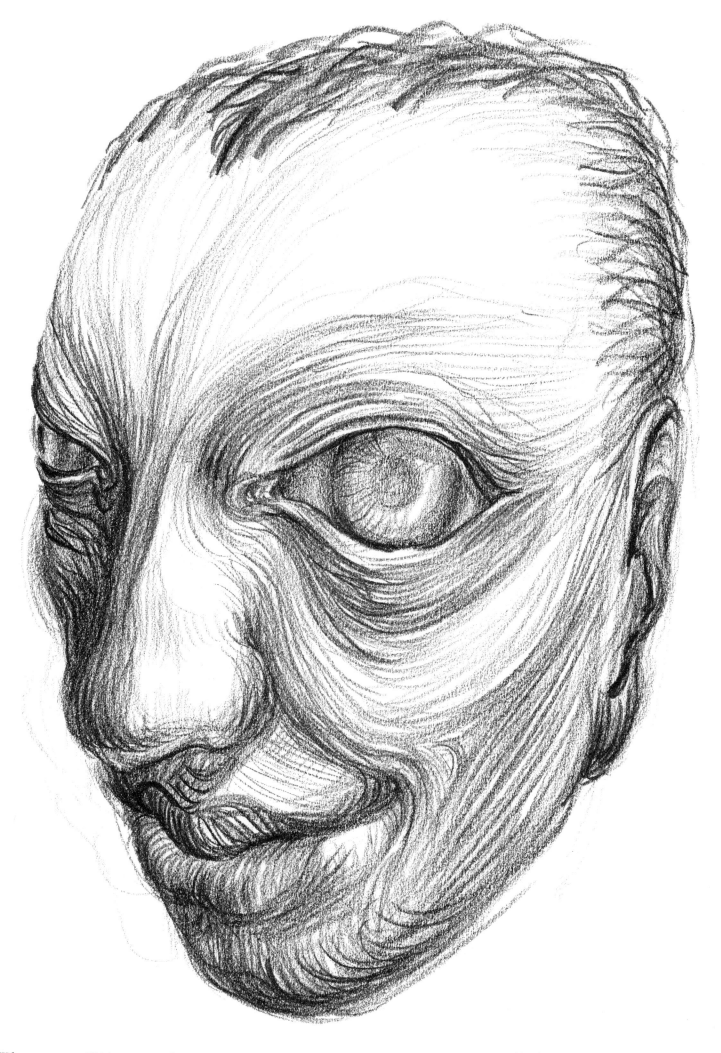

Wiley man   1944   pencil

Le roublard   1944   mine de plomb

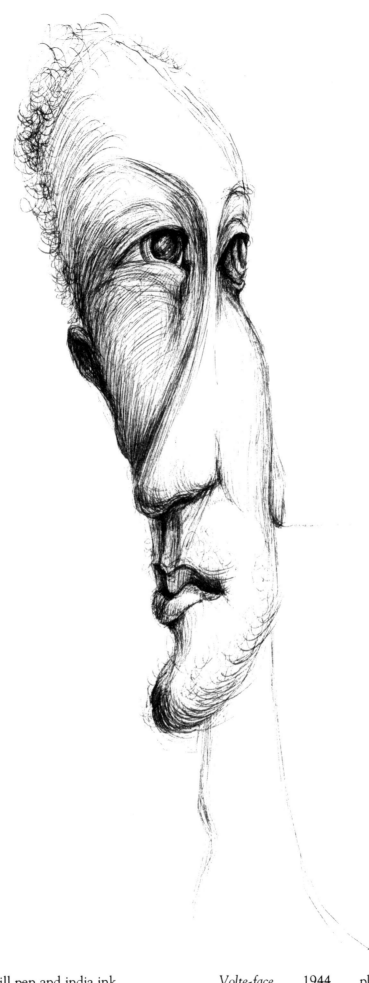

Turning head   1944   quill pen and india ink
Walking down Sparks Street, Ottawa, one day, I turned
back to look at someone who had passed me, only to find
that the someone also had turned back to look. I had the
strange feeling that not his neck had twisted but his head.

Volte-face   1944   plume d'oie et encre de Chine
Un jour que je déambulais rue Sparks, à Ottawa, je me
retournai pour jeter un regard sur un passant qui m'avait
croisé. Or le passant, lui aussi, s'était retourné et me
dévisageait. J'éprouvai la bizarre impression qu'il s'était
dévissé la tête sur le cou.

14

The backward glance   1945   quill pen and india ink   *Regard en arrière*   1945   plume d'oie et encre de Chine

Auschwitz undated pencil
I had seen my first movie shots of Auschwitz.

Auschwitz sans date mine de plomb
Je venais de visionner mes premières prises de vue de
Auschwitz.

Liberty arms herself   1943   pencil
I felt resentful at many of the things that were being done in the name of "Liberty."

La liberté armée   1943   mine de plomb
Je me sentais irrité par nombre d'abus commis au nom de la liberté.

Artists have expressed surrealism in many ways. For me it has meant that, in the first stages of a work, conscious motivation is surrendered, and the subconscious is allowed to break through and well up. This process can begin in a very small way. Just as a slip of the tongue may reveal the subconscious, so may a slip of the pen. The slip has to be allowed to have its own way, be nurtured and encouraged, until its activity has gained enough momentum for conscious control gradually to take over and mold the picture into some kind of unity.

Les artistes ont exprimé le surréalisme de bien des façons. Pour moi, il supposait une reddition de la motivation consciente, permettant ainsi au subconscient de percer et de jaillir. Souvent, par peu de choses au début: un trait de plume involontaire peut trahir le subconscient tout comme un lapsus. Cet automatisme, il faut le libérer, l'alimenter et l'encourager jusqu'à ce qu'il devienne assez résistant pour subir un contrôle graduel menant à une relative unité.

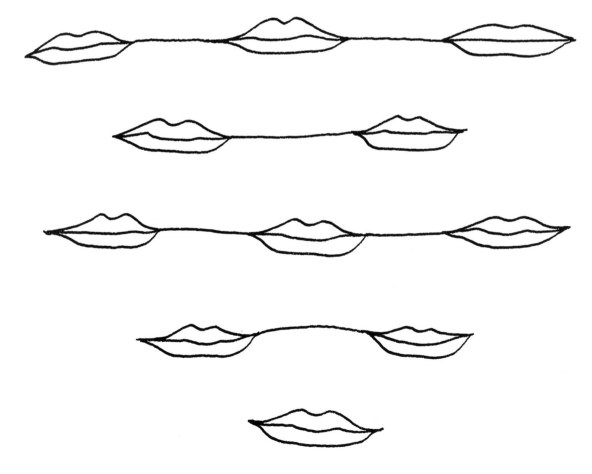

Lips   1963   pen and ink

Lèvres   1963   dessin à la plume

2

Surreal
drawings

Dessins
surréels

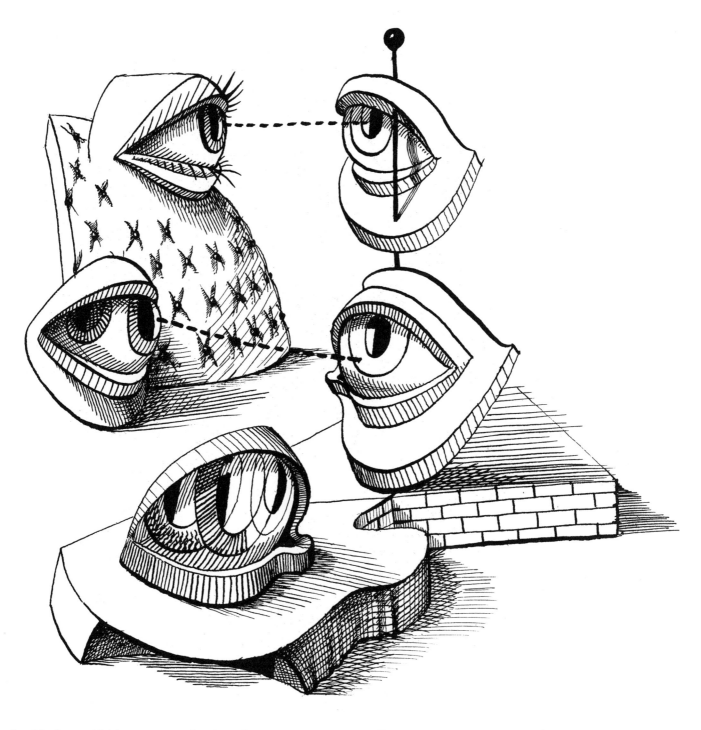

Having a hard look   1944   pen and india ink   *Regard sévère*   1944   plume et encre de Chine

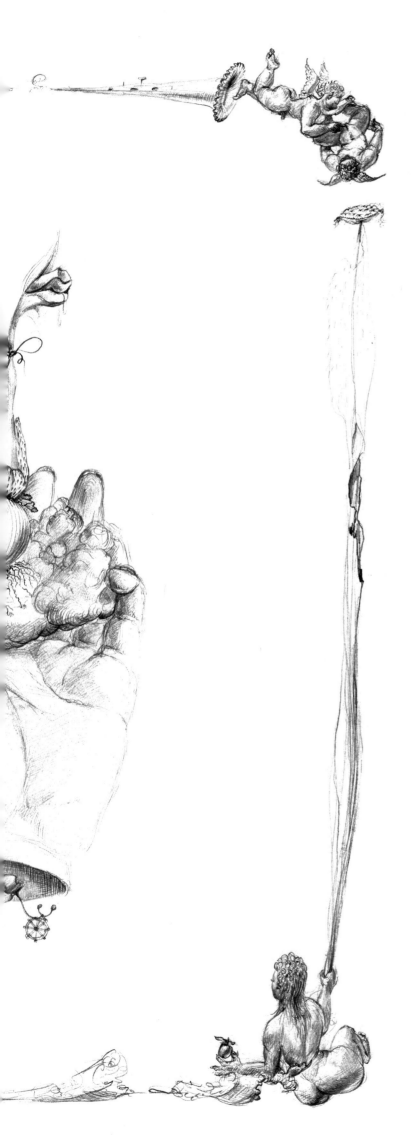

Haute cuisine   1943   pencil
With pencil I found it easier to convey sensuousness than with a pen.

Haute cuisine   1943   mine de plomb
Je trouvais plus facile de suggérer la sensualité avec le crayon plutôt qu'avec la plume.

untitled   1944   quill pen and india ink   sans titre   1944   plume d'oie et encre de Chine

untitled   1944   quill pen and india ink   sans titre   1944   plume d'oie et encre de Chine

St. George and the porcupine   1944   pencil
I dreamed of my friend George Dunning making love to a
porcupine. So vivid and strange was the dream that I had
to draw it. One often imagines one sees dreams in precise
detail. It's seldom so. Alas, the mechanism of this unusual
intercourse eluded me.

Saint-Georges et le porc-épic   1944   mine de plomb
J'ai rêvé que mon ami Georges Dunning faisait l'amour
avec un porc-épic. Rêve étrange mais si vivant qu'il m'a
fallu en faire un dessin. On s'imagine souvent avoir rêvé
des détails précis, mais c'est chose plutôt rare. Ainsi, la
technique de cet accouplement inusité m'a, hélas!,
complètement échappé.

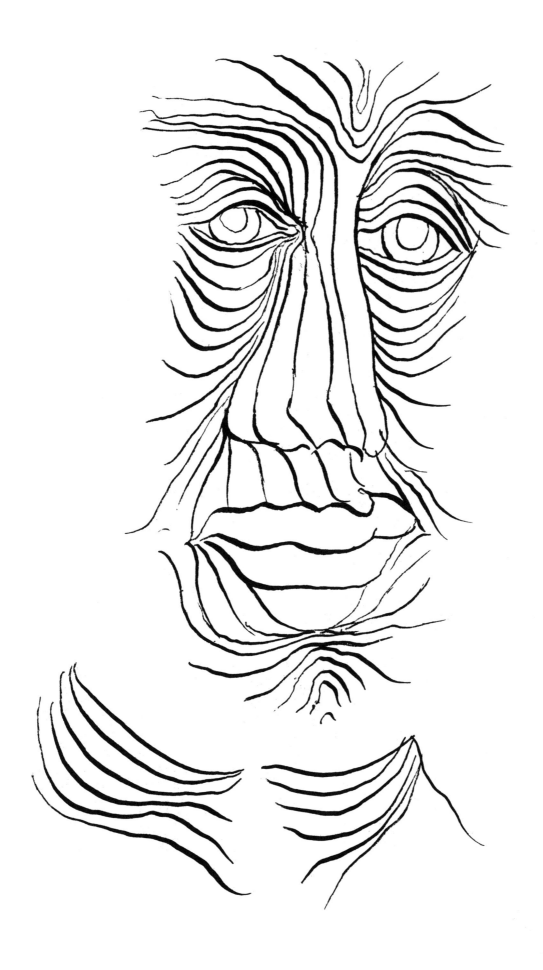

untitled   1946   quill pen and ink   sans titre   1946   plume d'oie et encre de Chine

Face on stairway   1946   quill pen and ink
For weeks I hadn't thought of a stairway and certainly
not uprooted features. I felt like drawing — but what?
Nothing came to mind, so I let my pen do what it wanted,
and this is what it wanted.

Un visage dans l'escalier   1946   plume d'oie et encre
de Chine
Il y avait des semaines que je n'avais pas pensé à un
escalier. Et surtout pas à une tête sans attache. J'avais
envie de dessiner, oui mais quoi? Rien ne me venant à
l'esprit, je laissai ma plume glisser sur le papier et voici ce
qu'elle me dicta.

Le coucou et l'alouette voudraient bien se marier
(Memory of the kiss)   1948   pencil

Le coucou et l'alouette voudraient bien se marier
(Souvenir d'un baiser)   1948   mine de plomb

28

Longing   1953   pencil

Nostalgie   1953   mine de plomb

The fragmented senses   1963   pen and india ink   *Les sens fragmentés*   1963   plume et encre de Chine

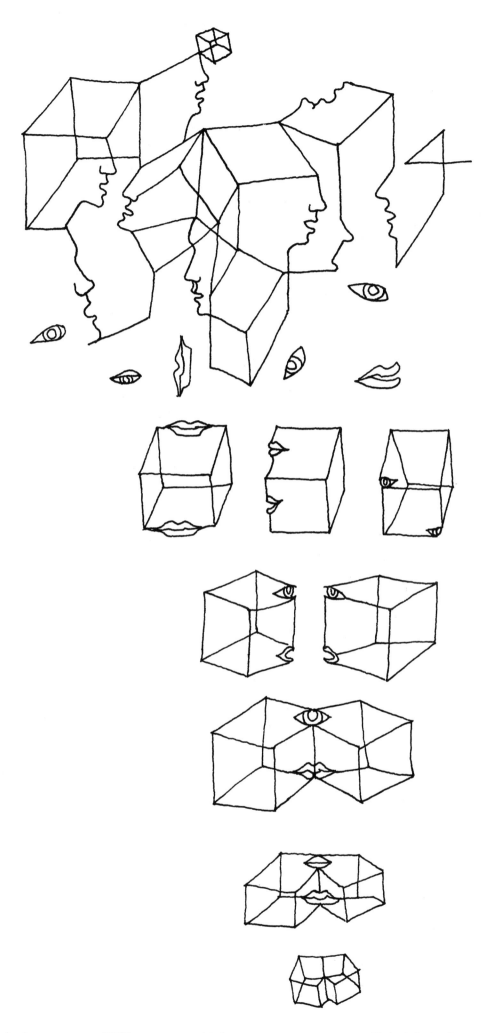

Face-cube fragments   1958   pen and ink
The progressive stages show the influence of film
animation.

Cube à faciès facetté   1958   dessin à la plume
On sent l'influence du film d'animation sur les étapes
progressives.

I've always had an interest in human faces and figures, which in no way conflicts with my fascination with abstractions; it is just the other end of the map. Sometimes I try to bring both ends together, but, I think, not too successfully.

Je me suis toujours intéressé au visage et au corps humain, ce qui en aucune façon ne contredit la fascination que j'éprouve pour l'art abstrait; un éventail peut être ouvert au maximum. J'essaie parfois d'en rapprocher les extrémités, mais sans beaucoup de succès, me semble-t-il.

untitled   1946   pen and inks
Done at a time when I was painting Canadian landscape for a Quebec folksong film and longing for that tropical island.

sans titre   1946   plume et encres
Exécuté à un moment où je peignais des paysages canadiens pour un film sur les chansons traditionnelles du Québec, tout en rêvant à mon île tropicale.

3

Faces and figures

Visages et figures

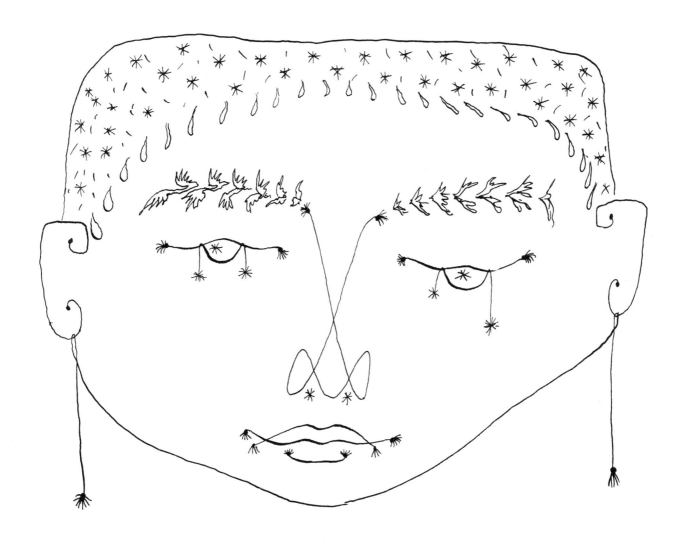

16 Sept 52

untitled   1952   quill pen and ink   sans titre   1952   plume d'oie et encre

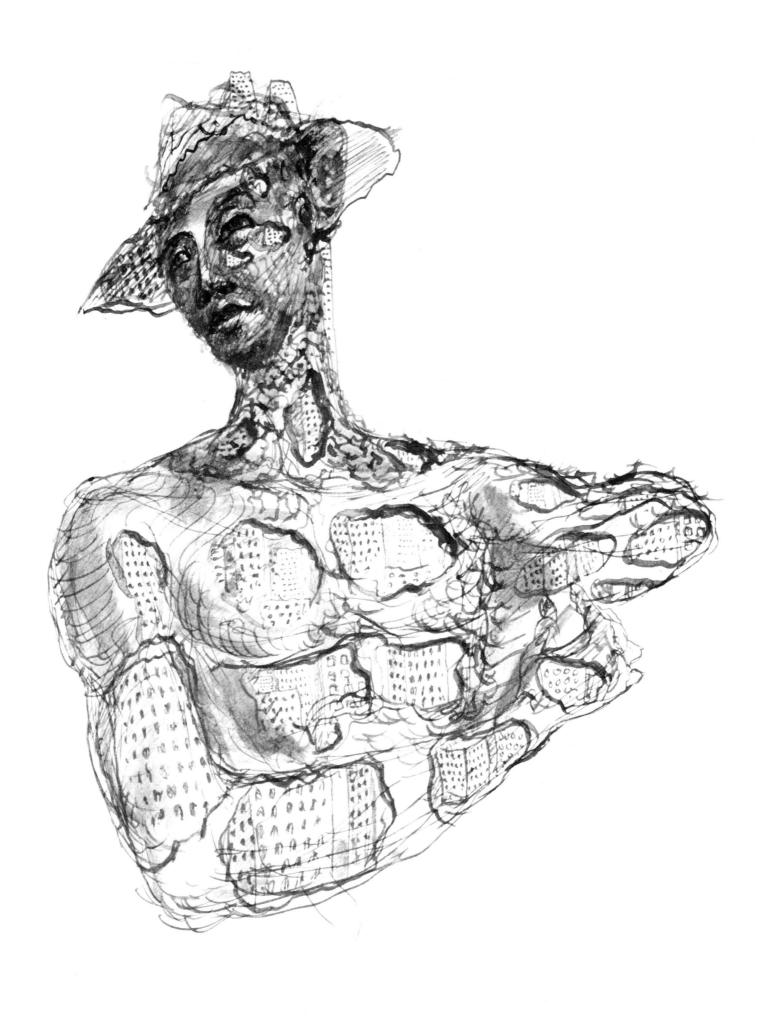

untitled   1946   pen, inks, wash
I had just come back from New York City, confused by noise, dirt and smoke, but wanting to go back.

sans titre   1946   plume et lavis
Je revenais de New York, ahuri par le bruit, la poussière et la fumée, mais voulant tout de même y retourner.

34

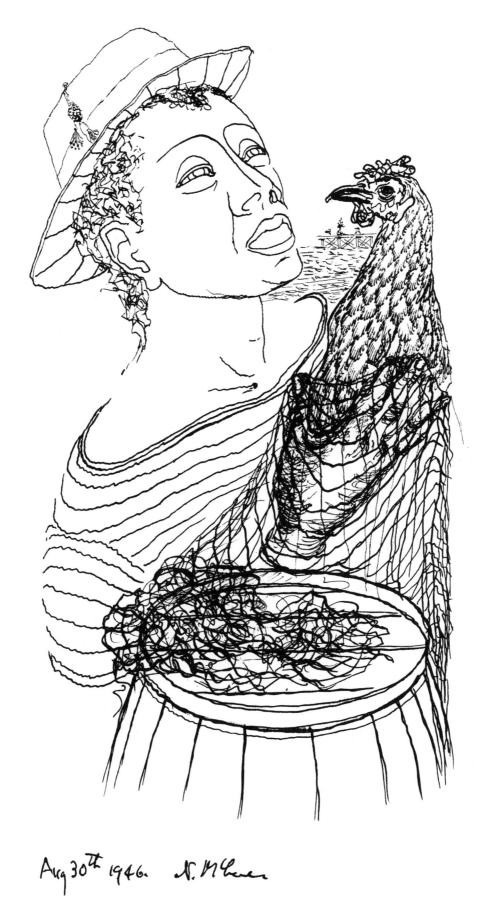

Aug 30th 1946. *N. M̃Cuen*

Sailor and bird   1946   pen and ink   *Le matelot et l'oiseau*   1946   dessin à la plume

More sailors, for Ernst   1949   quill pen and sepia ink   *Encore des matelots pour Ernst*   1949   plume d'oie et encre sépia

Sailor 1949 quill pen and sepia ink

Matelot 1949 plume d'oie et encre sépia

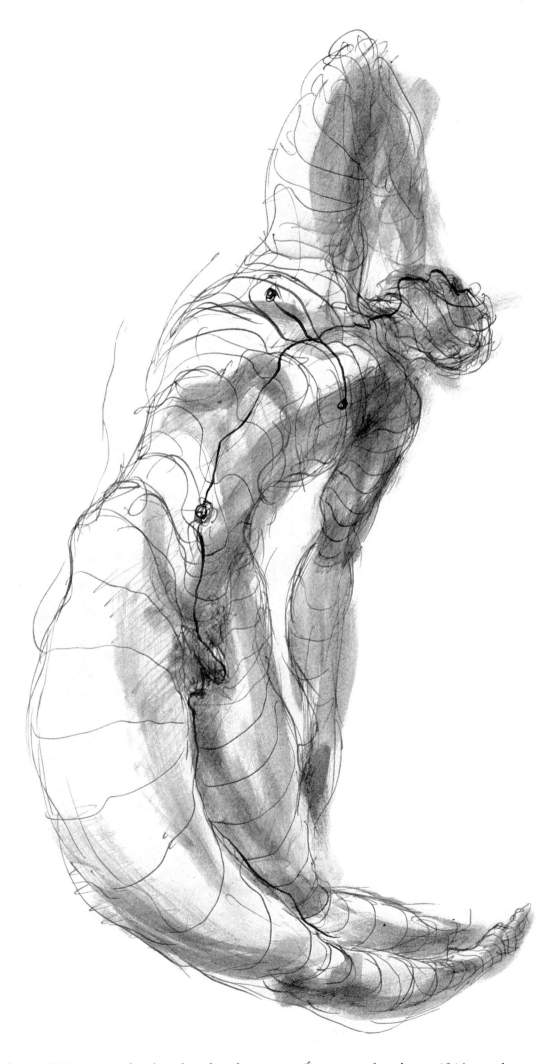

Wide-angle stretch 1946 pen, brush, ink and wash *Étirage grand angle* 1946 plume, pinceau et lavis

JAN 1948

Hermes 1948 pencil
About a year after doing this I realized I had lifted the idea
from a woodcut sent to me by Gertrude Hermes, an
English artist friend.

Hermes 1948 mine de plomb
Un an plus tard à peu près, je réalisai que l'idée m'en était
venue d'une gravure sur bois que m'avait envoyée
Gertrude Hermes, anglaise, artiste et amie.

Lust 1948 pencil
A subconscious drawing whose transparent significance I
realized only when I had completed it. A friend I was
longing to touch, but afraid to.

Lascivité 1948 mine de plomb
Dessin dont la signification subconsciente, et
transparente, ne m'est apparue seulement après l'avoir
terminé: le désir de toucher un ami mais sans oser faire le
geste.

39

Faces   undated   ball-pen
Studies from memory of people I had seen, or sat near.

Visages   sans date   stylo à bille
Études de mémoire de personnes entrevues ou auprès
desquelles je m'étais assis.

Memory of a Mexican beach   1957   dry brush   *Souvenir d'une plage mexicaine*   1957   pinceau sec

Interlocking faces   undated   soft pencil

Visages enclenchés   sans date   mine de plomb
(tendre)

16 Sept 52

untitled   1952   quill pen and ink

sans titre   1952   plume d'oie

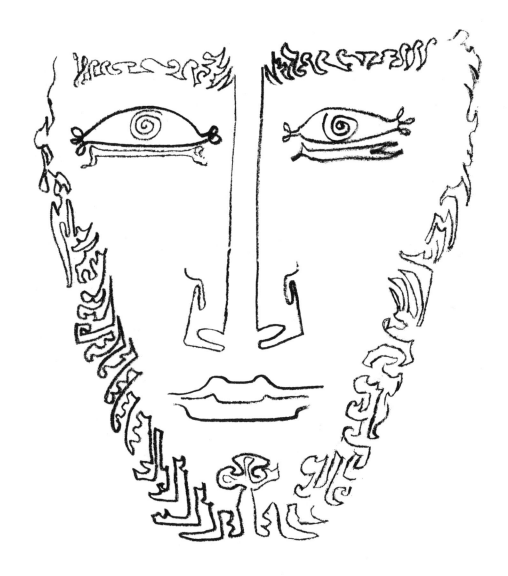

Stuart Legg   1953   colored crayon

Stuart Legg   1953   crayon de couleur

Invented faces   1964   pencil
They were done at a time when I was wanting to use the
pencil for rendering a kind of softness, tenderness, that
was my subject matter. Drawing with a pencil in this way,
so alien to pen and ink work, was like developing a
photograph in a darkroom.

 23 Sept 1964

Visages inventés   1964   mine de plomb
Exécutés à une période où je voulais employer la mine de
plomb pour exprimer une sorte de douceur, de tendresse
qui devenait le thème de mes dessins.

    Un tel rendu au crayon, tellement opposé au rendu à la
plume, me faisait penser au développement d'une
photographie en chambre noire.

I had been reading Russian fairy tales in a big book superbly illustrated by my friend Alexandre Alexeieff (whose film "Night on Bare Mountain" had influenced me greatly). These tales were more fantastic than Grimms' or other European ones. Moved by the stories and Alexeieff's illustrations I began using colored inks for the first time.

Je venais de lire des histoires de fées traduites du russe, dans un gros volume magnifiquement illustré par mon ami Alexandre Alexeieff dont le film "Night on Bare Mountain" m'avait grandement influencé. Ces contes étaient plus fantastiques que ceux de Grimm ou autres auteurs européens. Je fus remué par les contes et par les illustrations de Alexeieff et, à cette occasion, fis pour la première fois l'expérience des encres de couleur.

Pavilion   1946   pen and colored inks

Pavillon   1946   plume et encres de couleur

4

Fantasy

Fantaisie

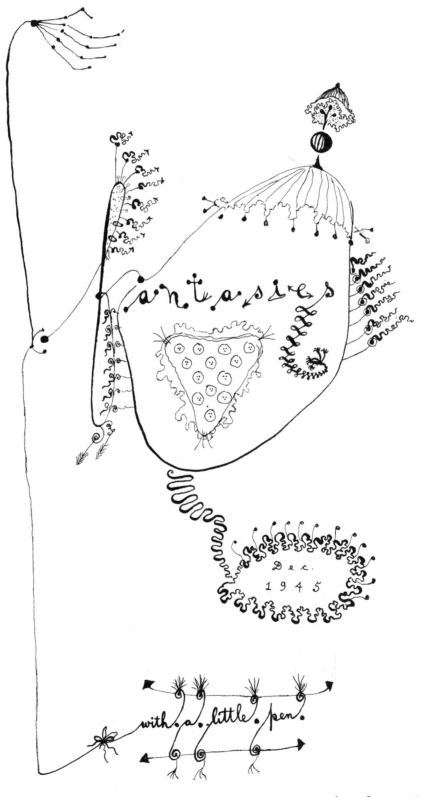

Fantasies with a little pen   1945   pen and colored inks

Fantaisies, plume fine   1945   plume et encres de couleur

untitled   1945   pen and colored inks

sans titre   1945   plume et encres de couleur

Xmas Eve 1945
after reading Russian Fairy Tales.

N McLuen

After reading Russian fairy tales   Christmas Eve   *Je venais de lire les contes de fées russes*   Veille de Noël
1945   pen and colored inks   1945   plume et encres de couleur

Norman
McLaren
Easter 1946.

An Easter Hen
walking in the garden
outside its house.

An Easter hen walking in the garden outside its
house   Easter 1946   pen and colored inks

Une poule de Pâques déambulant dans le jardin, devant le
poulailler   Pâques, 1946   plume et encres de couleur

Baba-Yaga in the Russian fairy tales   1945   pen and colored inks

Baba-Yaga dans les contes de fées russes   1945   plume et encres de couleur

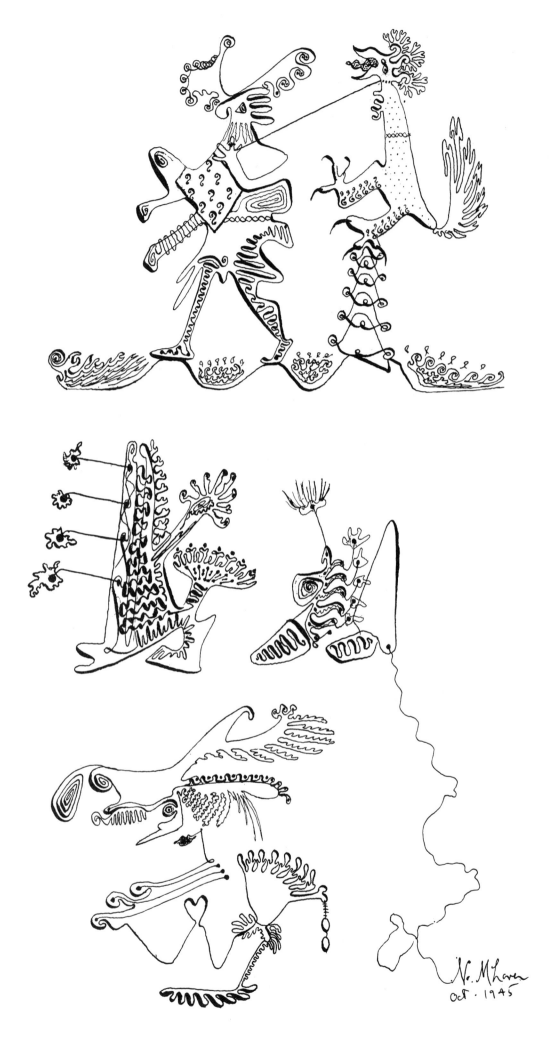

Crossing the stream   1945   pen and colored inks   *La traversée de la rivière*   1945   plume et encres de couleur

The formal kiss   1945   pen and colored inks

Le baiser de cérémonie   1945   plume et encres de couleur

Flying fantasy   1946   colored pencils
I had just bought a box of colored pencils, of a kind I hadn't used before, and was eager to try them out.

Fantaisie volante   1946   crayons de couleur
Je venais de m'acheter une boîte de crayons de couleur d'une marque que je n'avais jamais employée, d'où mon impatience de les essayer.

Chiaroscuro fantasy   1946   colored pencils   *Fantaisie en clair-obscur*   1946   crayons de couleur

Memories: Fig tree in Stirling Castle   1948   pen and
inks

Souvenir: un figuier dans le château Stirling
1948   dessin à la plume

N. McLaren

Nov. 1948

Memory of Scotland   1948   pen and ink
In these reminiscences of a trip to Scotland, I began
drawing precise details of the castle in my home town, but
soon found myself embroidering not only on the
architecture but on the memory of someone I met.

Souvenir d'Écosse   1948   dessin à la plume
Vu ces réminiscences d'un voyage en Écosse, je me suis
mis à dessiner des détails précis du château de ma ville
natale, mais bientôt je me mis à broder non seulement sur
l'architecture mais aussi sur le souvenir d'une rencontre.

Ever since I read about the great labyrinth at Knossos and visited the garden one at Hampton Court, I have been fascinated, even obsessed, by labyrinths. Though labyrinths were designed for the flat ground, I found myself sketching three-dimensional ones, with steps and stairs in all directions, criss-crossing, near-missing, dead-ending, curving back on themselves, and so on.

Once, after making an important irreversible decision in my life, I felt impelled to put doors in my labyrinths — doors that snapped shut behind one forever. But since then, my doors are not all like that; some might open onto Paradise. It is a bit like life, so many choices and doors and we don't know what lies behind them.

A labyrinth is a fascinating perambulatory puzzle. I would very much like to design and actually build one for people to amuse themselves in.

La lecture me renseigna sur le grand labyrinthe de Knossos et je visitai celui de Hampton Court. A partir de là, les labyrinthes sont devenus plus qu'une fascination pour moi: une obsession. Bien qu'il soient normalement conçus en surface, je me pris à en dessiner à trois dimensions, avec marches et escaliers multidimensionnels, en croisée ou en ne l'étant pas de justesse, en épingles à cheveux, sans issue, ou autres possibilités.

A la suite d'une importante et irrévocable décision que j'avais prise, je me sentis obligé d'ajouter des portes à mes labyrinthes, des portes qui, brusquement, se refermaient sur vous à jamais. Mais depuis, mes portes ne sont pas toutes de ce modèle; certaines peuvent déboucher sur le Paradis. C'est un peu comme dans la vie: toutes ces options, toutes ces portes. . . et nous ignorons ce qu'elles impliquent.

Un labyrinthe est une fascinante promenade-devinette. Il me plairait bien d'en concevoir et d'en réaliser un pour de vrai où les gens pourraient s'amuser.

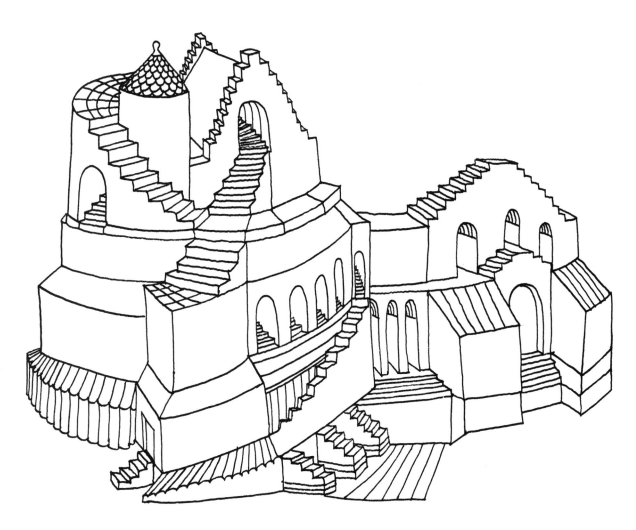

Scottish labyrinth   1963   pen and ink
After a trip to Rome, I think memories of the Coliseum became mixed up with my Scottish reminiscences.

Labyrinthe écossais   1963   dessin à la plume
À la suite d'un voyage à Rome, il semble que mes souvenirs du Colisée et ceux de l'Écosse se sont interpénétrés.

5

Steps
and doors

Portes
et escaliers

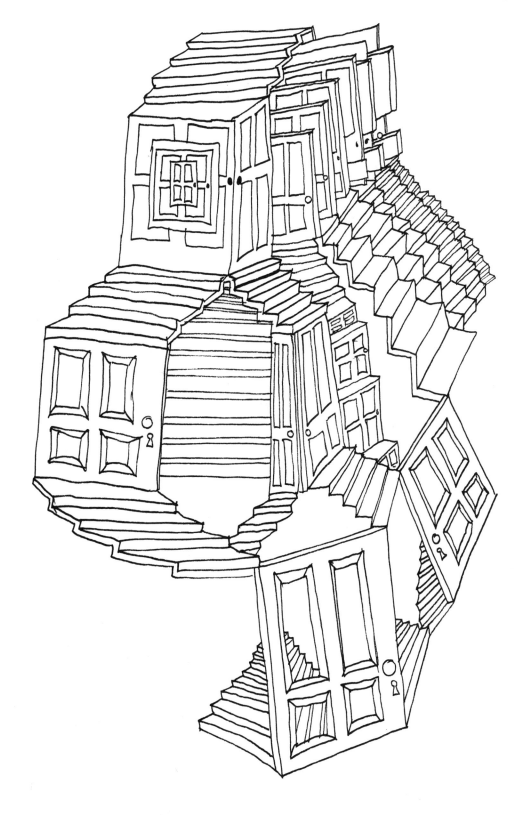

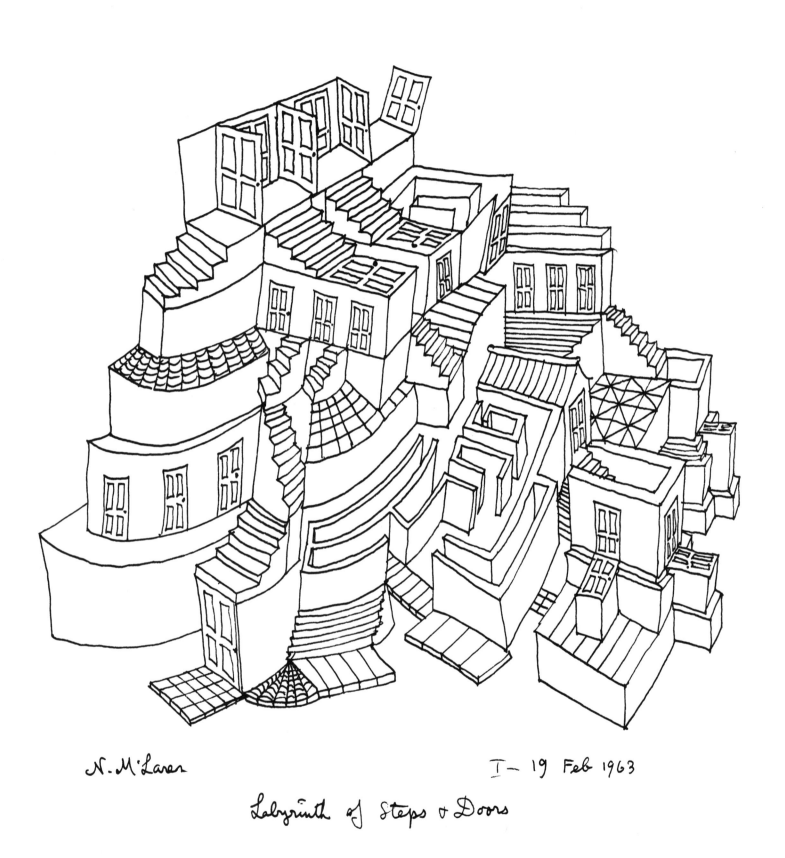

N. M'Laren   I— 19 Feb 1963

Labyrinth of Steps & Doors

Labyrinth of steps and doors   1963   pen and ink, original
Reminiscences of Scottish architecture and my interest in labyrinths seemed to coalesce in my mind.

Labyrinthe fait de portes et de marches   1963   plume et encre
Les réminiscences d'architecture écossaise et mon intérêt pour les labyrinthes ont semblé se confondre dans mon esprit.

N. McLaren

I— 19 Feb 1963

Labyrinth of Steps & Doors

Labyrinth of steps and doors   1963   ink on
reproduction

Labyrinthe fait de portes et de marches   1963   encre
par-dessus une reproduction

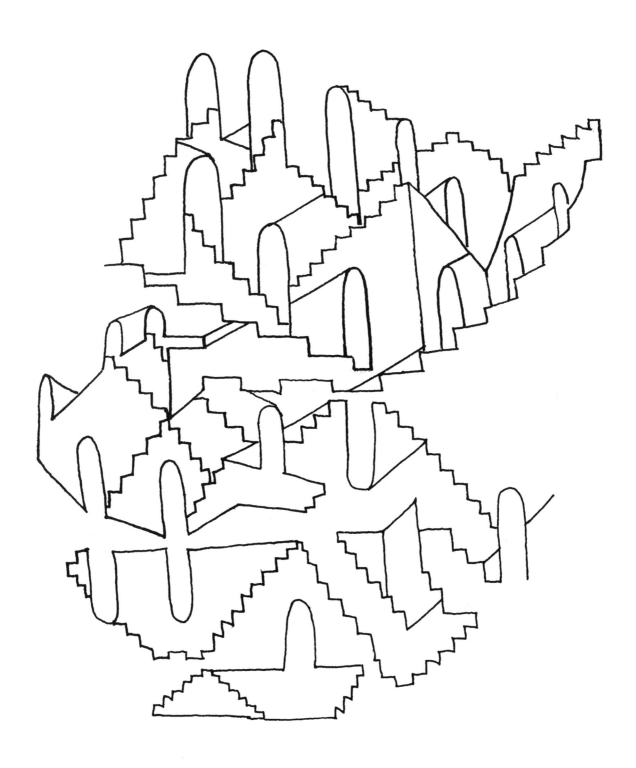

Steps and arches   1958   pen and ink
I began to make abstractions on the subject . . .

Gradins et arcades   1958   dessin à la plume
Je commençai par tirer des abstractions du sujet . . .

N. McL.

untitled   1964   pen and ink
. . . and then to make symbols with the theme.

sans titre   1964   dessin à la plume
. . . pour ensuite tirer des symboles du thème.

7 AUG 1963

Phallic drawing   1963   pen and ink   *Dessin phallique*   1963   dessin à la plume

1st (Oct.) Feb . 1963 —

NMℒ ,

Phallic drawing   1963   pen and ink

Dessin phallique   1963   dessin à la plume

I have always been interested in puzzles, particularly visual and spatial ones. Around 1950 my friend George Dunning got me excited about the four-dimensional cube, also called the hyper-cube or tesseract. We made many sketches, stereoscopic drawings and three-dimensional structures of it in balsa wood.

What exactly is a 4-D cube, or tesseract? What a point is to a line, a line is to a square; what a square is to a cube, a cube is to a tesseract.

Some of the tesseract's geometric properties can be worked out, for instance: a line is bounded by two points, a square by four, a cube by eight and a tesseract by sixteen. A line is held within two points, a square within four lines, a cube within six squares and a tesseract within eight cubes.

Depicting a cube (three dimensions) on a sheet of paper (two dimensions) is very similar to the problem of representing a tesseract (four dimensions) in solid space (three dimensions). In both cases, by an optical illusion, we create the impression of an additional but really fictitious dimension. Just as we can all, through habit, see flat line drawings as representing solid objects, so we can learn to see a solid "drawing" (structure) as the representation of a hyper-solid object; this is especially so with the simple form of a tesseract. In fact it is even possible to see some of a tesseract's properties on a flat drawing, as is done here.

Les devinettes, particulièrement les visuelles et les spatiales, m'ont toujours intéressé. Vers 1950, mon ami George Dunning excita ma curiosité au sujet des cubes à quatre dimensions, appelés aussi *tesseract*. Nous fîmes croquis, dessins stéréoscopiques et constructions quadri-dimensionnelles en bois de balsa.

Qu'est-ce, exactement, qu'un cube quadri-dimensionnel, ou *tesseract*? Ce qu'un point est par rapport à une ligne, une ligne à un carré; ce qu'un carré est par rapport à un cube, un cube l'est par rapport à un *tesseract*.

On peut définir quelques-unes des propriétés géométriques du *tesseract*. Exemple: une ligne est limitée par deux points, un carré par quatre, un cube par huit et un *tesseract* par seize. Une ligne est comprise entre deux points, un carré entre quatre lignes, un cube entre six carrés et un *tesseract* entre huit cubes.

Tracer un cube (tri-dimensionnel) sur une feuille de papier (bi-dimensionnel) est similaire au problème posé par la représentation d'un *tasseract* (quadri-dimensionnel) dans l'espace réel (tri-dimensionnel). Grâce à une illusion d'optique, nous pouvons, dans les deux cas, suggérer une dimension supplémentaire bien que fictive en réalité. Tout comme nous pouvons, par la force de l'habitude, voir des objets en relief alors qu'ils ne sont représentés que par des dessins au trait, nous pouvons apprendre à voir dans des solides la représentation de constructions en hyper-relief; c'est particulièrement vrai dans le cas de la forme simple du *tesseract*. En fait, il est même possible de voir certaines de ses propriétés dans un dessin au trait, tel que celui-ci.

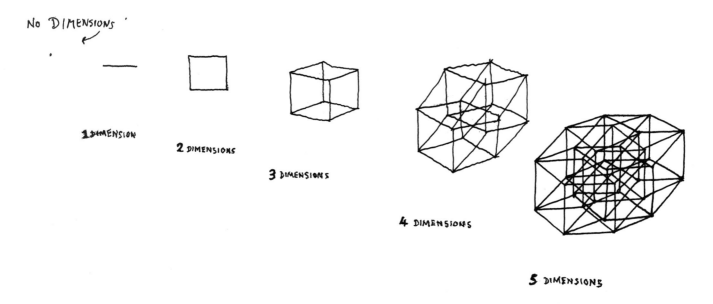

No DIMENSIONS

1 DIMENSION

2 DIMENSIONS

3 DIMENSIONS

4 DIMENSIONS

5 DIMENSIONS

ETC. →

One to six dimensions   undated   pen and ink   *De une à six dimensions*   sans date   dessin à la plume

6

Puzzles and mazes

Devinettes et labyrinthes

BIRDS STUDYING
SOLID GEOMETRY

N. M'Laren. May '58

Birds studying solid geometry   1958   pen and ink

Oiseaux étudiant la géométrie dans l'espace
1958   dessin à la plume

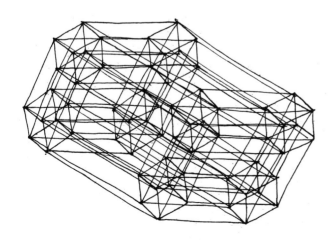

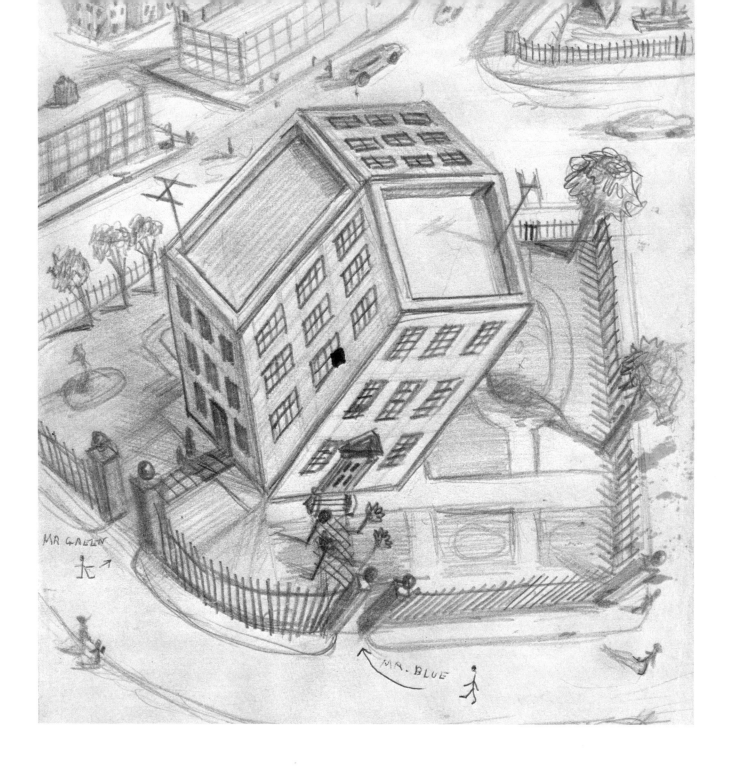

Tesseractine House   1953   pencil and colored crayon

Mr. Green and Mr. Blue lived in the same house — a four-dimensional house but, since they always stuck to their own entrances, each thought he lived in an ordinary 3-D house which abutted the other. People who live in semi-detached houses usually share a common wall, but Mr. Green and Mr. Blue shared a common set of rooms.

Mr. Green said the room with the blacked-out windowpane was on the ground floor; Mr. Blue said it was one flight up. When they were both in that room they'd have long arguments. Were they on the same floor at that moment — or was one of them one flight higher than the other?

And another bone of contention was the blacked-out windowpane. Was it a top pane, as Mr. Blue insisted? Or a bottom pane, as Mr. Green maintained? Moral: Only by seeing the whole picture can contradictions be resolved.

Maison quadri-dimensionnelle   1953   mine de plomb et crayon de couleur

M. Green et M. Blue habitaient la même maison à quatre dimensions. Comme ils s'en tenaient chacun à sa propre entrée, l'un et l'autre croyait habiter une maison jumelée à la voisine par un mur mitoyen alors qu'ils partageaient un ensemble de pièces communes.

M. Green prétendait que la pièce avec la fenêtre aveugle était située au rez-de-chaussée; M. Blue la plaçait à l'étage au-dessus. Quand ils se trouvaient ensemble dans cette pièce, ils avaient des discussions sans fin. Se trouvaient-ils au même étage à ces moments-là ou l'un d'eux était-il à l'étage au-dessus?

Autre sujet de controverse: le panneau qui bloquait la fenêtre était-il le panneau du haut — c'était là l'opinion de M. Blue — ou le panneau du bas comme l'affirmait M. Green?

La morale à tirer de tout cela, c'est que seule une vision globale permet de résoudre les contradictions.

all wheels spherical

Designs for 4-dimensional cars & bicycles

1953

Four-dimensional cars and bicycles 1953 pencil
People who live in four-dimensional houses should ride on four-dimensional bicycles (and should not throw four-dimensional stones!)

Voitures et bicyclettes quadri-dimensionnelles
1953 mine de plomb
Ceux qui habitent des maisons quadri-dimensionnelles ne devraient aller qu'à bicyclette de même conception et ne devraient pas jeter des pierres à quatre dimensions! (Note du tr.: Parodie du proverbe: People who live in glass houses should not throw stones.)

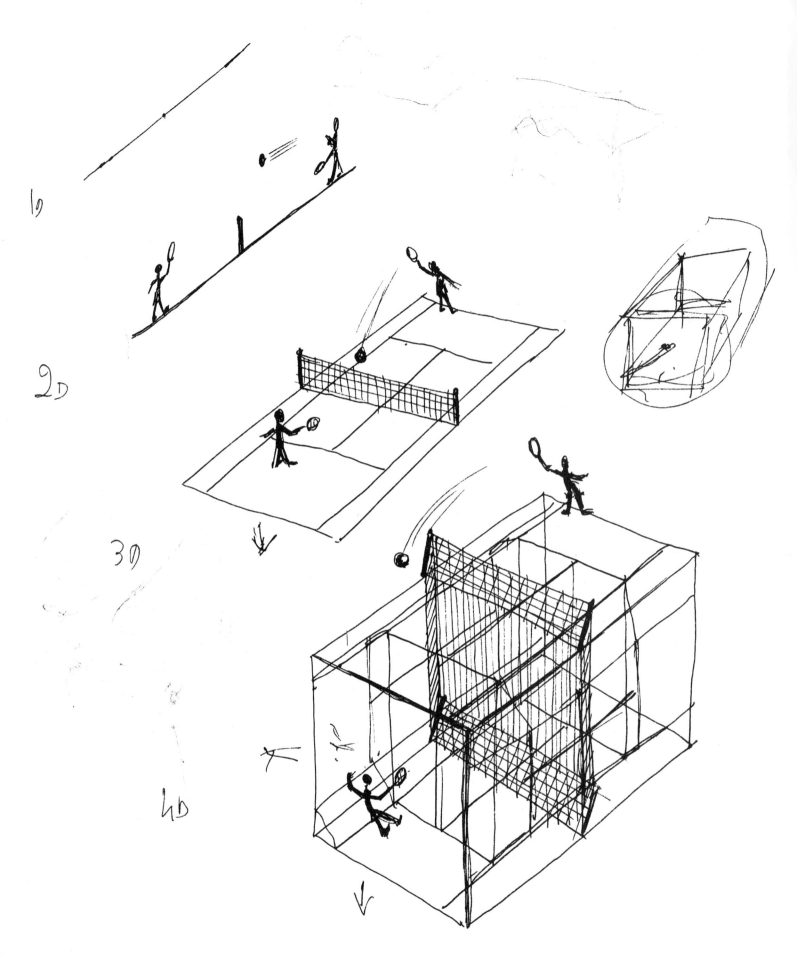

1D

2D

3D

4D

One, two, three and four dimensional tennis   undated
pen and ink
Using a spherical ball in a 4-D court is as incorrect as
using a wafer-thin disc in a traditional court. But how do
you represent a 4-D sphere? It's not as easy as a 4-D cube.

Tennis à dimension unique, à dimensions doubles,
triples et quadruples   sans date   dessin à la plume
Ne pas employer une balle sphérique sur un terrain
quadri-dimensionnel; ce serait aussi incorrect qu'employer
un disque de l'épaisseur d'une crêpe suzette sur un court
traditionnel. Mais comment représenter une balle 4 d.?
Un cube 4 d. n'offre pas autant de difficultés.

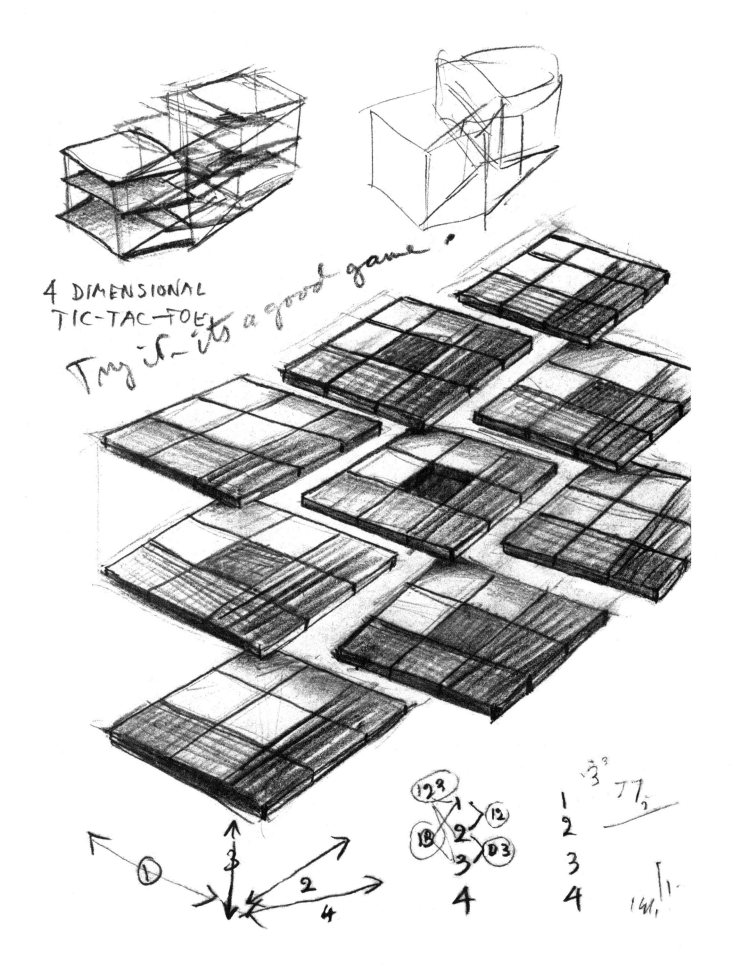

4 DIMENSIONAL
TIC-TAC-TOE
Try it — it's a good game!

Four-dimensional tic-tac-toe 1952-1953 pencil and crayon
In 1952 and 1953 at the Film Board we made a 3-D and then a 4-D tic-tac-toe game. Of course nowadays 3-D tic-tac-toe is a game you can buy. Playing games on a structure like this exercises the imagination, even strains it.

Tic-tac-toe 4 d. 1952-1953 mine de plomb et crayon de couleur
A l'Office du film en 1952 et 53, nous avons fait un jeu de tic-tac-toe 3 d. puis un jeu 4 d. On trouve maintenant, bien sûr, des jeux 3 d. dans le commerce. Un jeu ainsi structuré exerce l'imagination et même exige un effort.

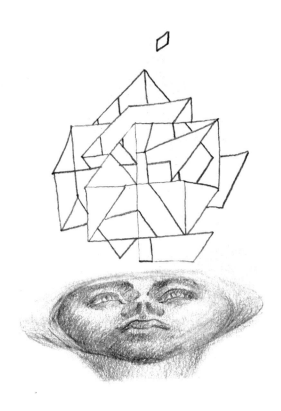

Women studying optical contradictions   1964   pencil,
pen, ink

Dames étudiant des contradictions optiques
1964   plume et mine de plomb

Men studying optical contradictions   undated   pencil
A structure? contradiction? illusion? or trick?

Messieurs étudiant des contradictions optiques   sans date   mine de plomb
Relief? Contradiction? Illusion? Attrape?

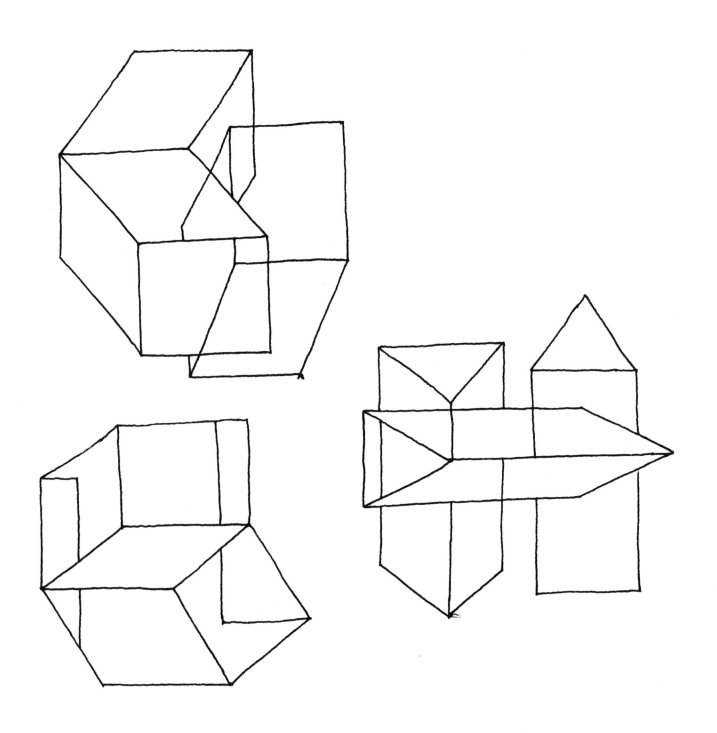

THREE CONTRARY OBJECTS   N. 24 June 58.

Three contrary objects   1958   pen and ink   *Trois objets contradictoires*   1958   dessin à la plume

A *contrastructory hen* 1958 pen and ink

Une poule contrastructurée 1958 dessin à la plume

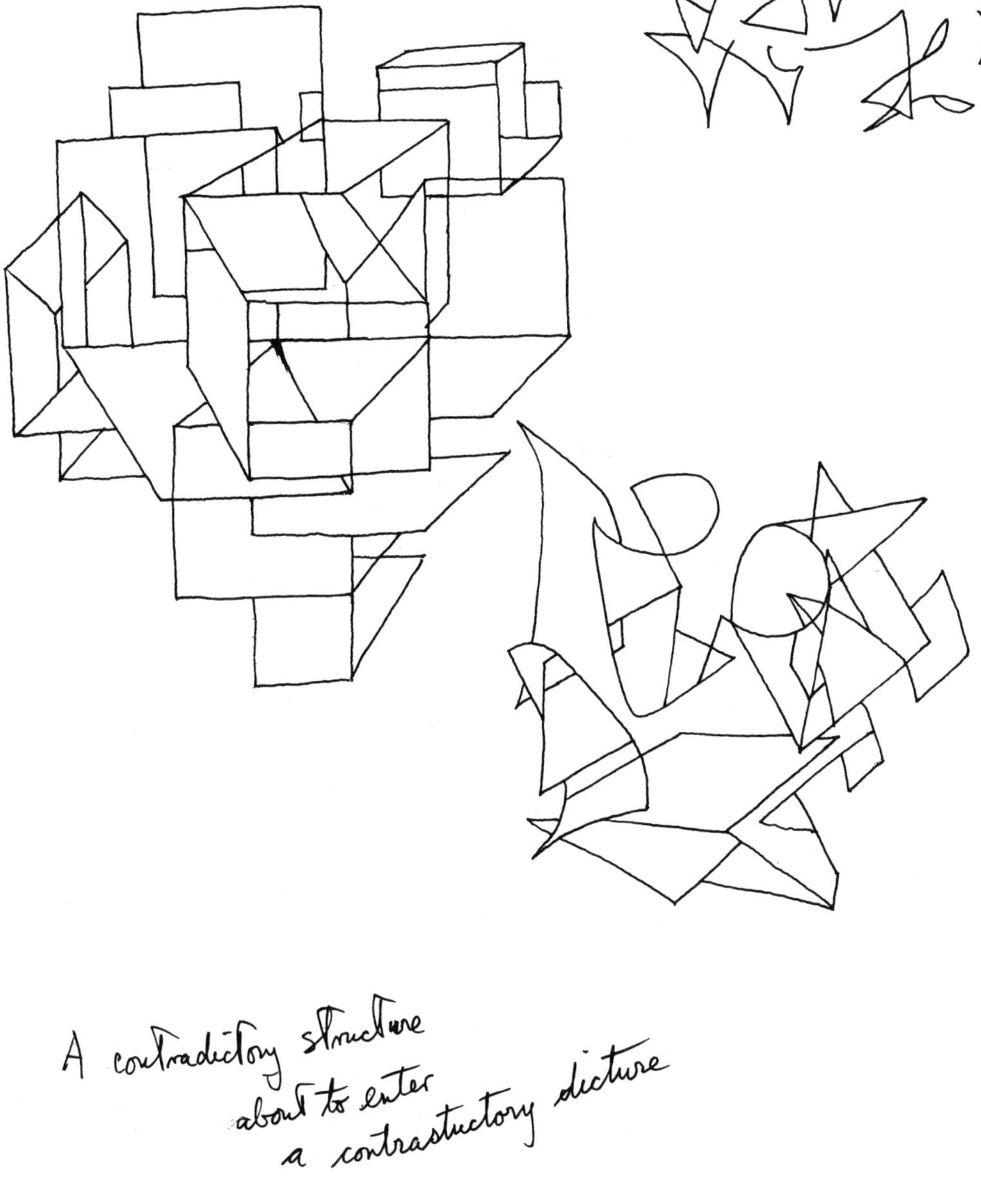

A contradictory structure
about to enter
a contrastructory dicture

A contradictory structure about to enter a contrastructory
dicture 1958 pen and pencil

*Structure contradictoire sur le point de pénétrer une dicture
contrastructurelle* 1958 plume et mine de plomb

A *maze* 1952 pencil

Labyrinthe 1952 mine de plomb

MAZE

July 52

Maze 1952 pencil
The idea of a maze has always intrigued me. I have made
a lot of plans. I would like to build one with pleasant
compensations for people who get lost or come to dead
ends: compensations like comfortable seats and benches,
unusual plants or flowers, fish ponds, fountains, pieces of
sculpture, etc.

Dédale 1952 mine de plomb
Le principe même du labyrinthe m'a toujours intrigué. J'ai
étudié bien des possibilités. J'aimerais en construire un qui
offrirait des compensations agréables aux gens égarés ou
dans une impasse: des sièges ou des bancs, par exemple,
des plantes ou des fleurs rares, des aquariums, des
fontaines, des sculptures, etc.

Illusion labyrinth   1965   pen and ink   *Labyrinthe illusoire*   1965   dessin à la plume

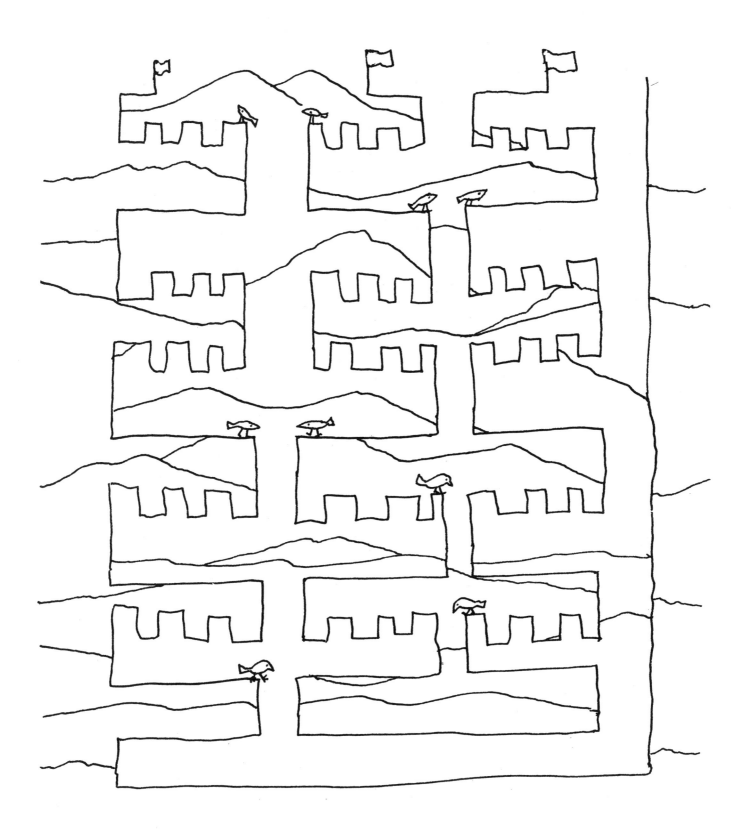

Winter birds   1966   pen and ink

Oiseaux d'hiver   1966   dessin à la plume

81

(Done when working on a mercator and other projections of the globe.)   1946   quill pen, brush and ink
The total surface of the globe can be represented on a flat surface — why can't a human head, which is roughly spherical? This was my first attempt.

(Exécuté en travaillant sur des projections de Mercator et autres projections du globe.)   1946   plume d'oie et pinceau
La surface du globe peut être représentée sur une surface plane. Pourquoi pas la tête humaine, plus ou moins sphérique de forme? Voici mon premier essai.

Portrait

Portrait 1946 quill pen and ink
Depicting heads according to certain types of map projection fascinated me.

I was also experimenting with wide interocular stereoscopic viewing devices and built one with about twenty-four inches between the right and left eye (instead of the usual two-and-a-half). I would look at friends, close up, with my eyes virtually twenty-four inches apart. The effect stunned me.

Portrait 1946 plume d'oie
Dessiner une tête selon certains procédés cartographiques me fascinait.

J'ai fait des essais avec des dispositifs interoculaires et stéréoscopiques. L'un avait environ vingt-quatre pouces entre l'oeil droit et l'oeil gauche (au lieu des deux pouces et demi réels). Je pouvais voir de mes amis en gros plans avec une distance virtuelle de vingt-quatre pouces entre les deux yeux. L'effet était stupéfiant.

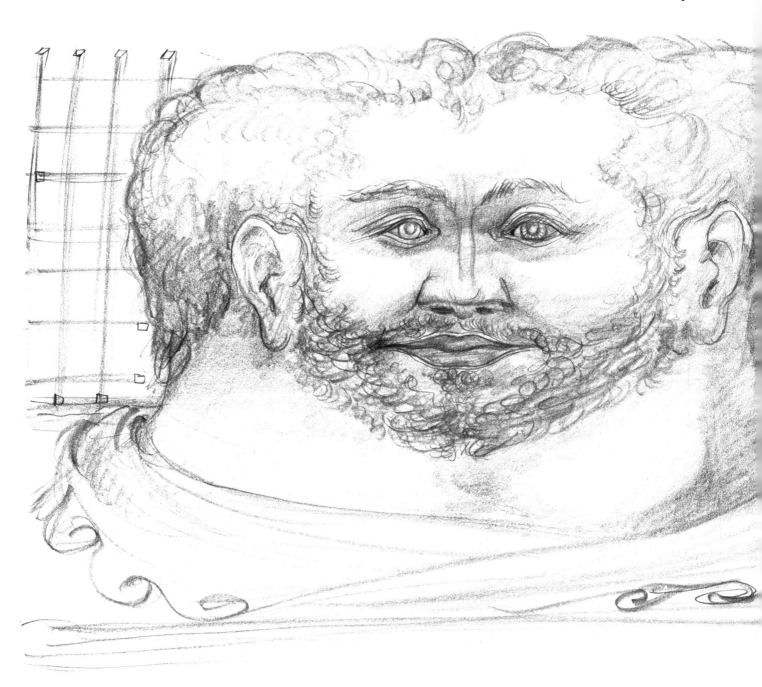

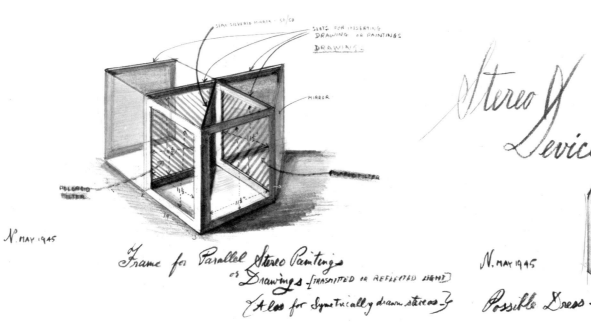

Stereo devices   1945   pencil

sans titre   1946   mine de plomb

July 20th 1946

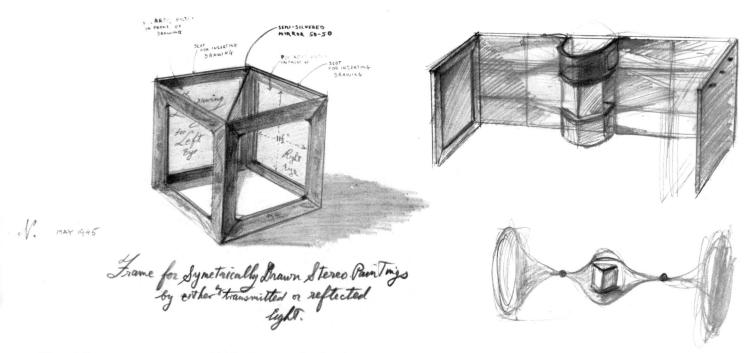

Dispositifs stéréoscopiques   1945   mine de plomb

My visit to China made a great impression on me. I went there for UNESCO to teach young Chinese artists to make filmstrips on village hygiene. Soon after I arrived, the Red Army took over our village; they let us continue to work. What I saw under the new regime warmed my faith in humanity again.

I had no time to draw for myself, but the fabulous mountains of central China burned themselves into my memory. When I returned to Canada, that landscape was a recurring theme in my drawings.

Mon premier séjour en Chine m'impressionna grandement. Sous les auspices de l'Unesco, j'enseignai à de jeunes artistes chinois à faire de courts métrages sur "l'hygiène au village". Peu après mon arrivée, l'armée rouge s'empara du village, mais nous laissa continuer notre travail. Ce que j'observai sous le nouveau régime ranima ma foi dans l'humanité.

Je ne trouvai pas le temps de dessiner, mais les fabuleuses montagnes de la Chine centrale se gravèrent dans ma mémoire. A mon retour au Canada, ce paysage revenait sans cesse dans mes dessins.

untitled   undated   dry brush

sans titre   sans date   pinceau sec

7

China   La Chine

Town on Yangtze   undated   pen and wash   *Petite ville au bord du Yangtze*   sans date   plume et
lavis

untitled   undated   brush and ink

sans titre   sans date   pinceau et encre

untitled   undated   pen, brush, ink and wash   sans titre   sans date   plume, pinceau et lavis

untitled   undated   pen, brush, ink and wash   sans titre   sans date   plume, pinceau et lavis

Town passed by on the Yangtze.

NcMhewer 1954
SUMMER

Town passed by on the Yangtze   1954   ink with pen
and wash

Petite ville vue du Yangtze   1954   plume et lavis

19 AP. 1964

Near Peh-Pei   1964   pen with ink and wash

Près de Peh-Pei   1964   plume et lavis

Central China   1950   pen and ink   *La Chine centrale*   1950   dessin à la plume

Memory of town on Yangtze River, 1950

Memory of town on Yangtze River   1950   pen and wash

Dessin de mémoire d'une ville au bord du Yangtze
1950   plume et lavis

Islands

1954 SUN=

Islands   1954   pen, brush and wash   *Iles*   1954   plume, pinceau et lavis

The metamorphosis of one shape or form by gradual stages into another shape or form is an important feature of film animation. It led me to think of putting the various stages side by side on a sheet of paper, rather than on a series of film frames. I was aware the idea was not new. I remember how intrigued I had been when I first saw the metamorphosing imagery of the nineteenth-century French illustrator Granville.

La métamorphose d'un contour ou d'une forme devenant graduellement un autre contour ou forme est une caractéristique importante du film d'animation. Il me vint à l'idée de juxtaposer les différents états d'un dessin animé sur une feuille de papier plutôt que dans une série de cadrages. Je savais bien que l'idée n'en était pas nouvelle. Je me rappelle combien l'imagerie à métamorphose de Granville, un illustrateur du 19ᵉ siècle, excita ma curiosité la première fois que j'en pris connaissance.

Border for invitation to Montreal Interenational Film Festival   1965   pen and ink

Bordure d'invitation du Festival international du film de Montréal   1965   dessin à la plume

8

Metamorphy

Métamorphie

Sun metamorphy   undated   pen and ink

Soleil et métamorphie   sans date   dessin à la plume

Doodle   undated   pen and ink   *Gribouillis*   sans date   dessin à la plume

Sketches for film "Là-haut sur ces montagnes"   1945   Esquisses pour le film "Là-haut sur ces montagnes"   1945

Movie film creatures   1962   pen and ink

Créatures de film cinématographique   1962   dessin à la plume

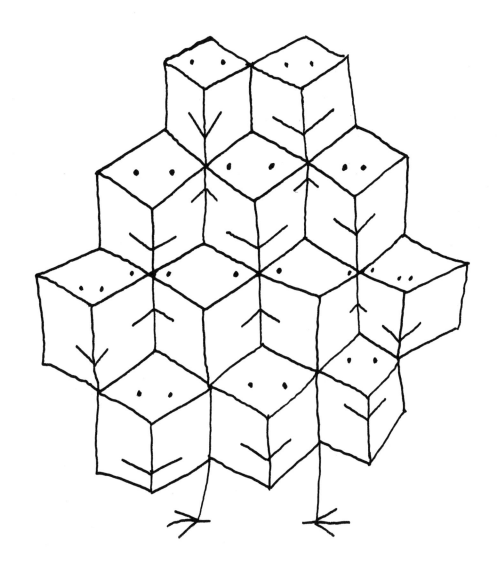

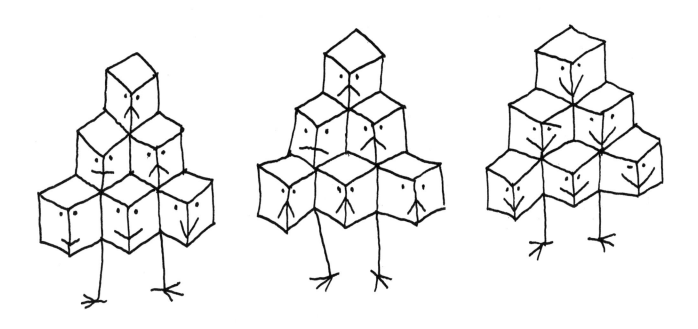

Cube creatures   1962   pen and ink   *Créatures en forme de cubes*   1962   dessin à la plume

untitled   undated   pen and ink

sans titre   sans date   dessin à la plume

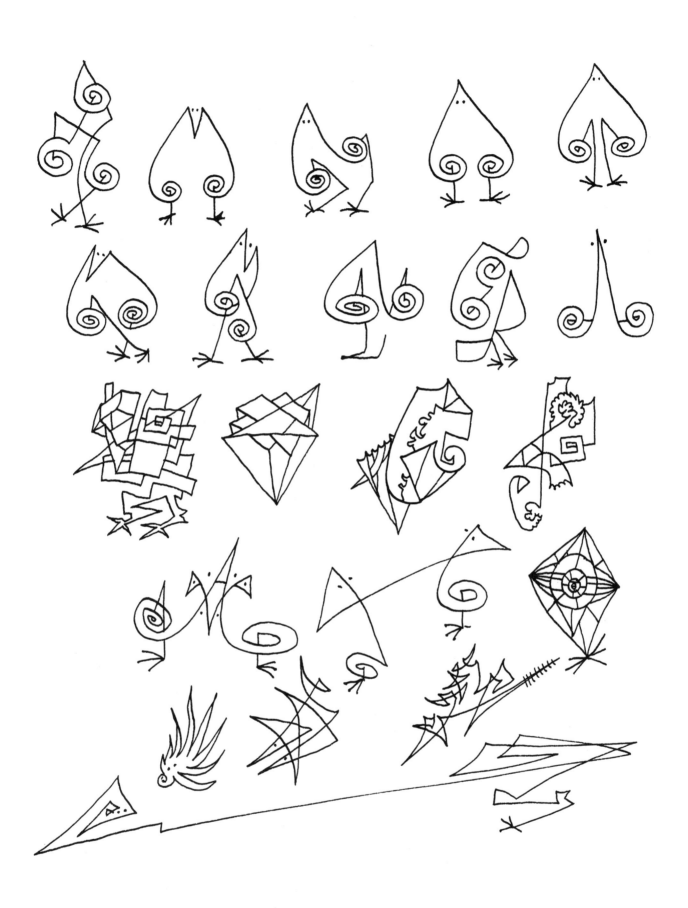

Miscellaneous creatures   1962   pen and ink   Créatures diverses   1962   dessin à la plume

Metamorphy   1963   pen and ink   *Métamorphie*   1963   dessin à la plume

Wings started appearing in my first animated film "Love on the wing," made for the British Postal Air Service in 1938; then birds and chickens. I had a period when I was crazy about hens. I studied them at the Experimental Farm in Ottawa, in a henhouse with over a thousand hens in it. As they weren't used to an artist sitting in their house, I caused a great fluster and panic and a chorus of hysterical cackling. Gradually they calmed down, and I felt I had been accepted. When I imitated their clucking and they came up to me, I knew I had. I was mainly interested in catching their movements and postures.

C'est dans mon premier film d'animation "Love on the wing", commandé par British Postal Air Service en 1938, que je commençai à me servir du motif des aigles; puis ce fut le tour des oiseaux et des poules. Pendant un temps, les poules m'emballèrent. Je les ai étudiées à la Ferme expérimentale d'Ottawa, dans un poulailler qui en logeait un millier. Elles n'avaient certes pas l'habitude de voir un artiste dans leur enceinte: je fus cause d'agitation, de panique et de caquettante hystérie. Elles finirent par se calmer, ce qui me donna l'impression d'être accepté. J'en eus la confirmation quand mon caquet d'imitation les attira vers moi. Ce qui surtout m'intéressait, c'était de saisir leurs mouvements et leurs attitudes.

Anatomical studies of hen's feet   1946   pencil

Etude anatomique des pattes de poule   1946   mine de plomb

9

Birds and other creatures

Des oiseaux et autres créatures

untitled   Bindated   pen and ink   sans titre   sans date   dessin à la plume

untitled   1958   pen and ink   sans titre   1958   dessin à la plume

108

Birds   1958   pen and ink

Des oiseaux   1958   dessin à la plume

untitled   undated   pen and ink   sans titre   sans date   dessin à la plume

untitled   1958   pen and ink   sans titre   1958   dessin à la plume

Birds   undated   pen and ink   *Oiseaux*   sans date   dessin à la plume

SIX BIRDS HAVING A DISCUSSION

Six birds having a discussion (A jury of six birds, Cannes)
1958   pen and ink
I was on the short film jury at Cannes in 1958. In our final deliberations we sat around trying to be wise. It reminded me of a lot of old owls, but each, in his own way, couldn't quite live up to the traditional character of this bird.

Discussion à six oiseaux (Un jury de six oiseaux à Cannes)   1958   dessin à la plume
Je fis partie du jury des courts métrages à Cannes, en 1958. Au cours des délibérations ultimes, nous étions là, à jouer les sages, et cela me fit penser à un tas de vieux hiboux. Mais nous ne pouvions, en tout état de cause, faire honneur à la réputation que la tradition prête à ces oiseaux.

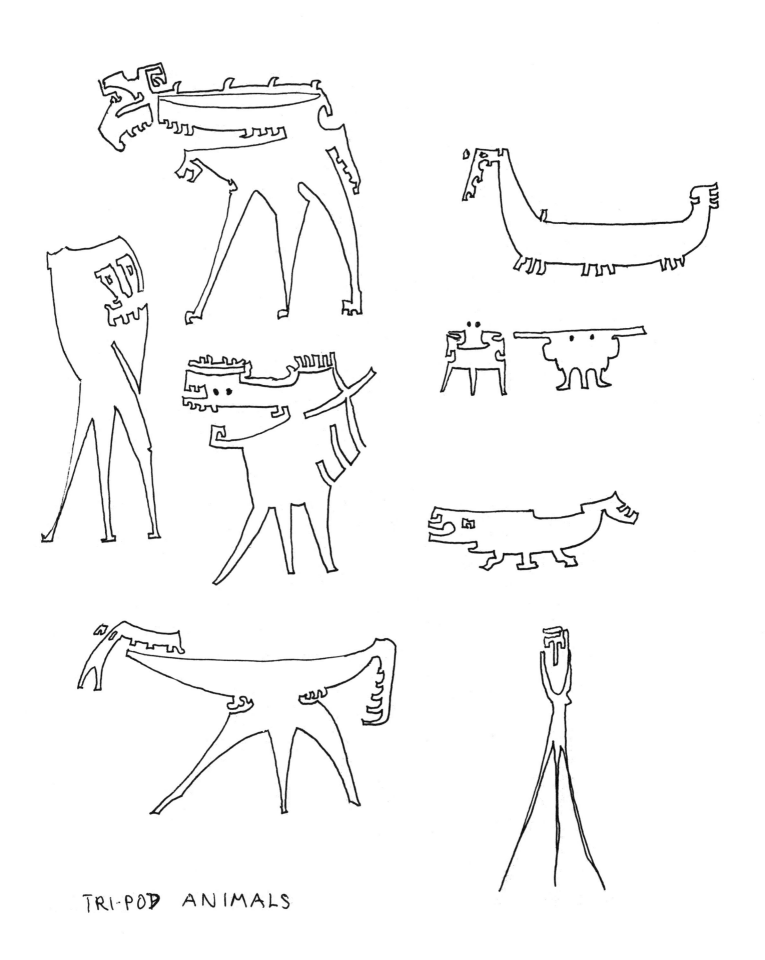

TRI-POD ANIMALS

Tripod animals   undated   ball-pen

Animaux tripèdes   sans date   stylo à bille

113

Bowing and scraping   1958   pen and ink   Salamecs et courbettes   1958   dessin à la plume

Aristocrat   1958   quill pen and ink

Aristocrate   1958   plume d'oie

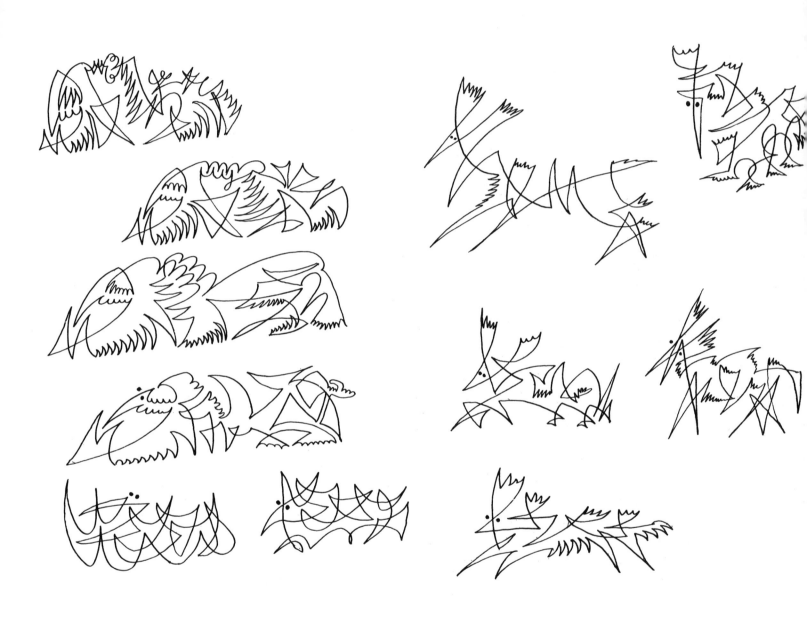

untitled   undated   pen and ink

sans titre   sans date   dessin à la plume

March 1952

N McGan

untitled   1952   pen and ink

sans titre   1952   dessin à la plume

118

Confused animal ↗

Demented animal ↑

N M₂.

March 1952

Animals   1952   quill pen and ink

Animaux   1952   plume d'oie et encre

Attack   undated   pen and ink

Attaque   sans date   dessin à la plume

PLAYING CATS CRADLES

N. M°Laren. Oct 58

Playing cat's cradles   1958   pen and ink

Pratiquant le jeu du berceau   1958   dessin à la plume

OCT 58

Cat's cradle   1958   pen and ink   *Le jeu du berceau*   1958   dessin à la plume

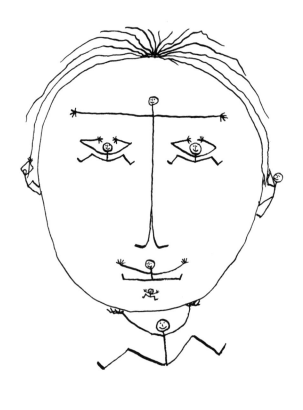

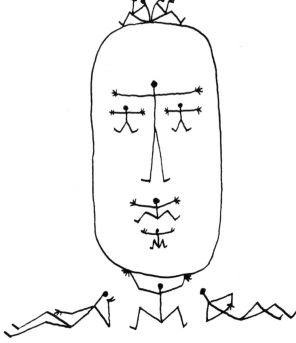

Mannikins 1952 pen and ink

Mannikins 1952 dessin à la plume

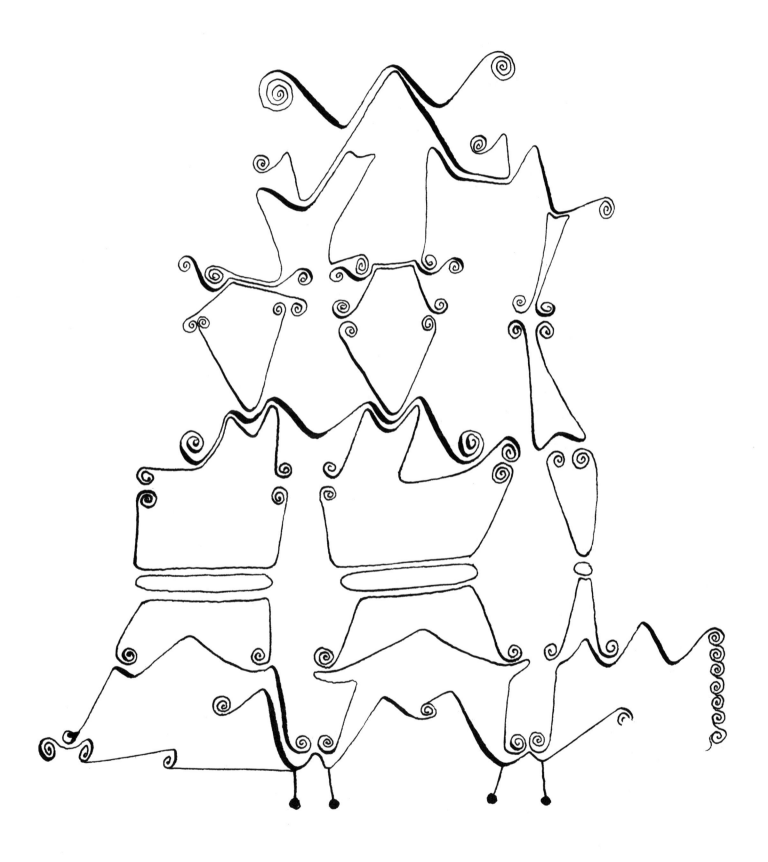

Greek animal   1946   pen, red and black ink   *Animal grec*   1946   dessin à la plume et aux encres
rouge et noire

Sometimes when sending personal letters to friends and acquaintances, I would have difficulty expressing myself in words. So I got into the habit of doing a fancifully drawn letter with little images and a minimum of written matter. On one such occasion I started a letter, which, due to the combination of a very high wind and my being drunk, had neither images, words, nor sense, but only a suggestion of wind. It led to the idea of drawing "abstract" and "semi-abstract" letters — usually to myself.

Il m'est arrivé d'éprouver quelque difficulté à m'exprimer par des mots en écrivant à des amis ou connaissances. J'ai donc pris l'habitude de rédiger mes lettres avec peu de mots et de les compléter avec de petits dessins fantaisistes.

Il m'est arrivé de commencer une de ces lettres alors que j'étais ivre et qu'il ventait très fort. De cette conjonction ne résultèrent ni mots, ni images, ni cohérence, seulement une impression de vent. D'où l'idée qui m'est venue d'écrire des lettres "abstraites" ou "semi-abstraites", et généralement adressées à moi-même.

N   1955   brush, pen and ink

N   1955   plume et pinceau

10

Letters

Lettres

A letter about landscape   undated   pen and ink   *Lettre à propos d'un paysage*   sans date   dessin à la plume

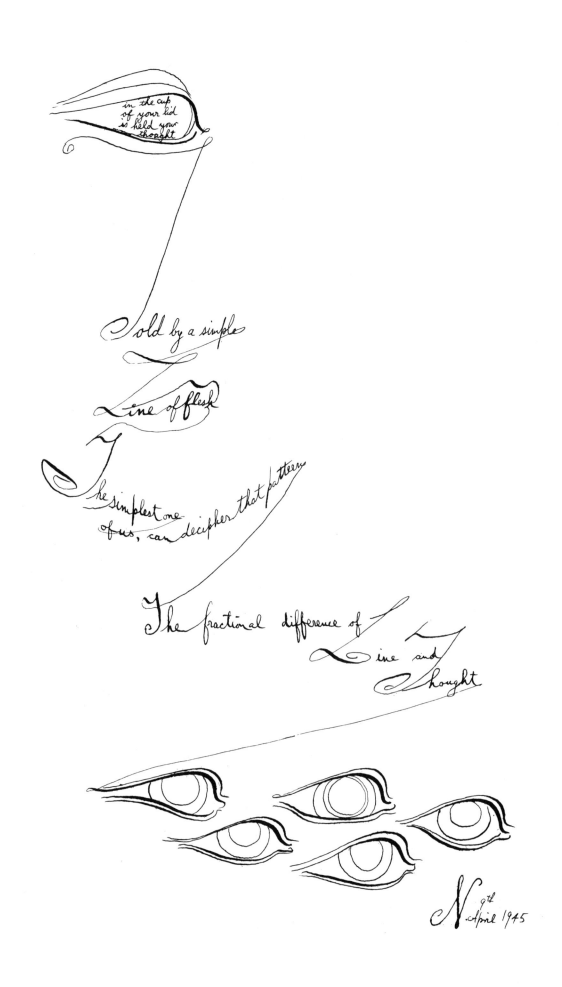

In the cup
of your lid
is held your
thought

Told by a simple

Line of flesh

The simplest one
of us, can decipher that pattern

The fractional difference of
Line and
Thought

N. 9th April 1945

Calligraphic verse 1945 pen and ink
I never got farther than this with the idea of interweaving
written matter and images.

Un vers calligraphique 1945 dessin à la plume
Je voulais entremêler vocables et illustrations, mais la
tentative n'alla pas plus loin.

520 St Patrick St
Ottawa.
July 1945

My Dear Hermes

I dont know how to express my delight and joy with what you have sent

Letter to Gertrude Hermes   1945   quill pen and ink
An English artist had given me a beautiful woodcut. I wanted to send her a nice letter and this is how I began. But feeling I could do better, this became only the start of a first draft.

Lettre à Gertrude Hermes   1945   plume d'oie
Cette artiste britanique m'avait fait don d'une belle gravure sur bois et je voulais lui envoyer une lettre gentille. En voici un début. Mais je croyais pouvoir faire mieux. Il s'agit donc du commencement d'un premier brouillon.

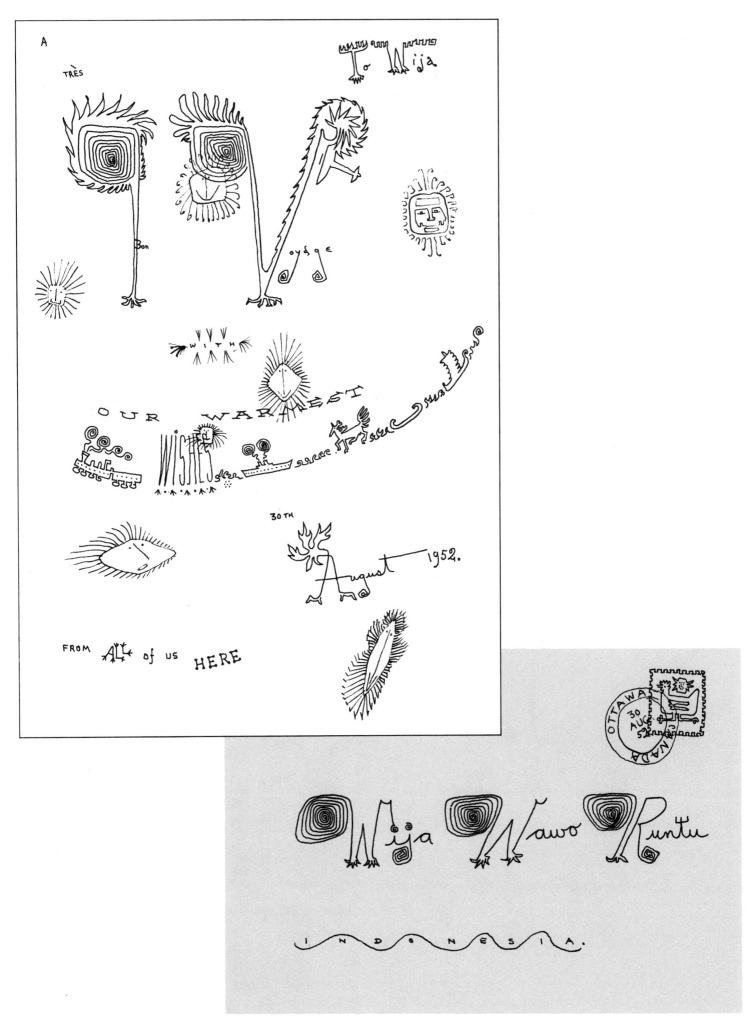

Letter and envelope 1952 pen and colored inks
A farewell letter to an Indonesian friend who was leaving
the Film Board.

Lettre et enveloppe 1952 plume et encre de couleur
Lettre d'adieu au nom d'un ami indonésien quittant
l'Office du film.

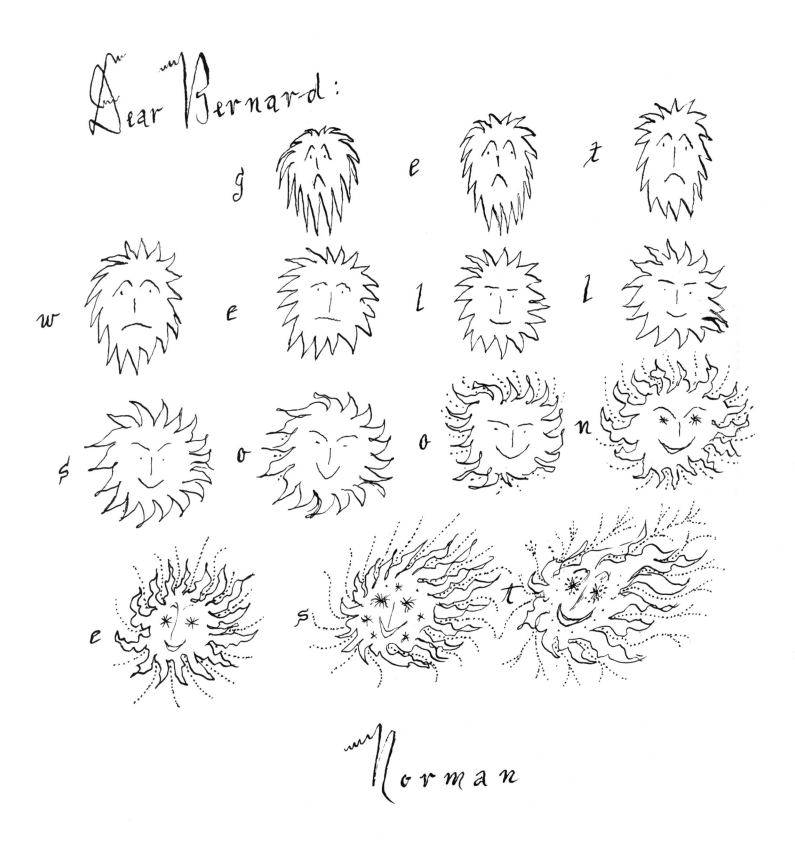

18 November 1960

Dear Bernard:

g e t w e l l s o o n e s t

Norman

Letter to Bernard   1960   pen and ink
My friend Bernard Gross was ill. I wanted to cheer him up.

Lettre à Bernard   1960   dessin à la plume
Mon ami Bernard Gross étant malade, j'ai voulu le réconforter.

Montreal, 11-XI-60.

Dear André Tahon

The world you created last night was miraculous, superb, and utterly enchanting. May I express my humble admiration for your great artistry.

Norman McLaren

Letter to André Tahon after a theatrical performance at the
Film Board in Montreal   1960   pen and ink

Lettre à André Tahon à la suite d'un spectacle de théâtre à
l'Office national du film à Montréal   1960   dessin à la
plume

A letter for the birds   1962   pen and ink   *Lettre pour les oiseaux*   1962   dessin à la plume

Gossipy letter, two pages   1952   quill pen

Lettre de potins de deux pages   1952   plume d'oie

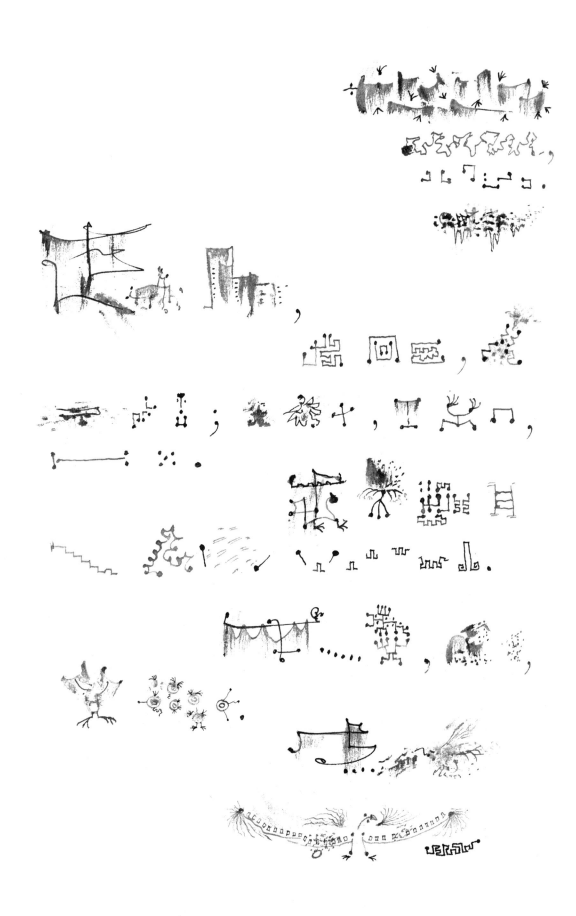

Letter   undated   brush, pen and ink

Lettre   sans date   pinceau, plume et encre

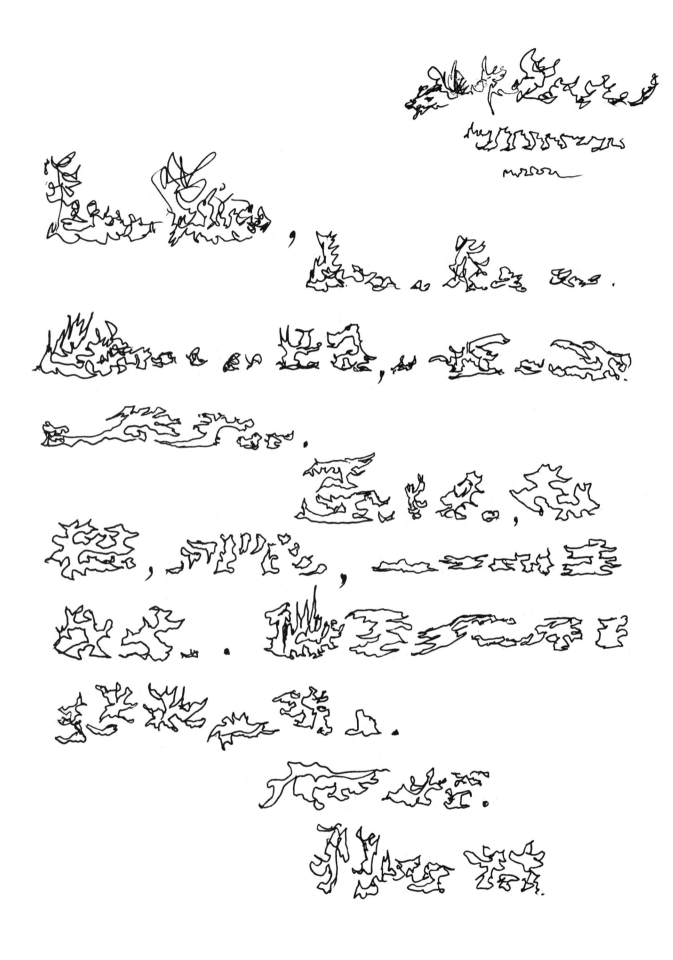

Letter   undated   ball-pen

Lettre   sans date   stylo à bille

A letter in a high wind (to Willard) 1958 pen and ink

Une lettre pleine de vent (adressée à Willard) 1958 dessin à la plume

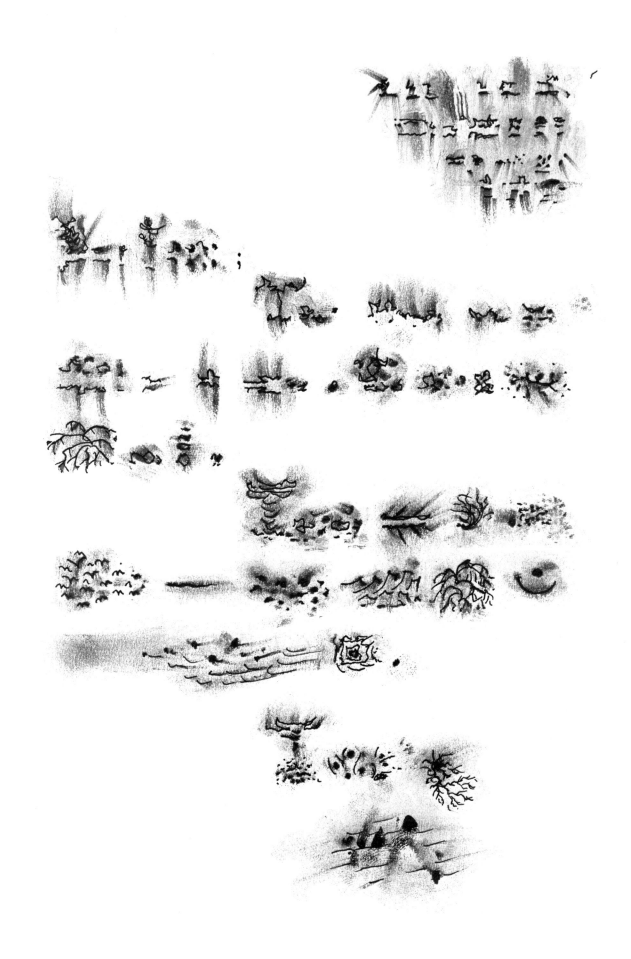

Letter   undated   pen and smudged ink   *Lettre*   sans date   plume et taches d'encre

Letter   undated   brush and wash

Lettre   sans date   pinceau et lavis

Letter   undated   brush, pen and ink

Lettre   sans date   pinceau, plume et encre

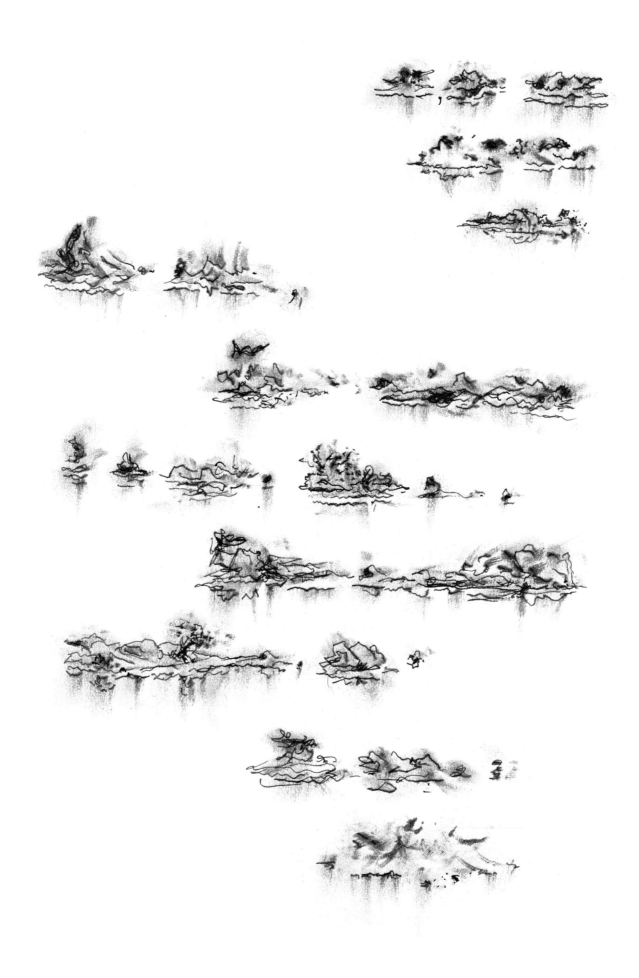

Letter   undated   pen and smudged ink

Lettre   sans date   plume et taches d'encre

A letter about islands   1964   pen and smudged ink
(collection of the National Gallery, Ottawa)

Lettre sur les îles   1964   plume et taches
d'encre   (collection du Musée national à Ottawa)

Letter   undated   brush, pen and ink

Lettre   sans date   pinceau, plume et encre

142

Letter   undated   brush and ink   *Lettre*   sans date   pinceau et encre

Around 1960 I became fascinated by pears, Bosc pears. First it was just to eat them, then it was to admire their shapes.

At the supermarket I would spend much time at the pear counter, carefully choosing the finest forms. Back home they were eaten in order of shapeliness, the least intriguing first. As pears of this kind ripen suddenly — too hard one day, perfect the next and gone the third — it was always a great problem trying to balance my aesthetic and gastronomic interests. Usually the best pears went bad. I couldn't bear to eat them.

Then I started drawing pears, and painting pears. I was obsessed by pears — but pleasantly obsessed. They were not symbols; it was their shape. And it wasn't other pears, only Bosc.

Vers 1960, j'éprouvai comme une fascination pour les poires, plus exactement, les poires Bosc. Au début pour leur goût et, par la suite, pour leur forme. Je passais beaucoup de temps au comptoir des poires du supermarché à choisir les plus belles de contour. De retour chez moi, je les classais à ma manière, en commençant par manger les moins attrayantes. Cette sorte de poires mûrissent soudainement: trop dures aujourd'hui, parfaites demain, trop mûres après-demain. En conséquence de quoi se posait toujours le sérieux problème d'essayer d'équilibrer art et gastronomie. Les plus belles poires souvent se gâtaient: je ne pouvais me résoudre à les manger.

Puis je me mis à dessiner des poires et à les peindre. C'était devenu une obsession, mais une agréable obsession. Nulle recherche de symbole; seule leur forme m'intéressait. Encore fallait-il que ce fût exclusivement des poires Bosc.

Pears   1960   pencil

Poires   1960   mine de plomb

11

Pears

Poires

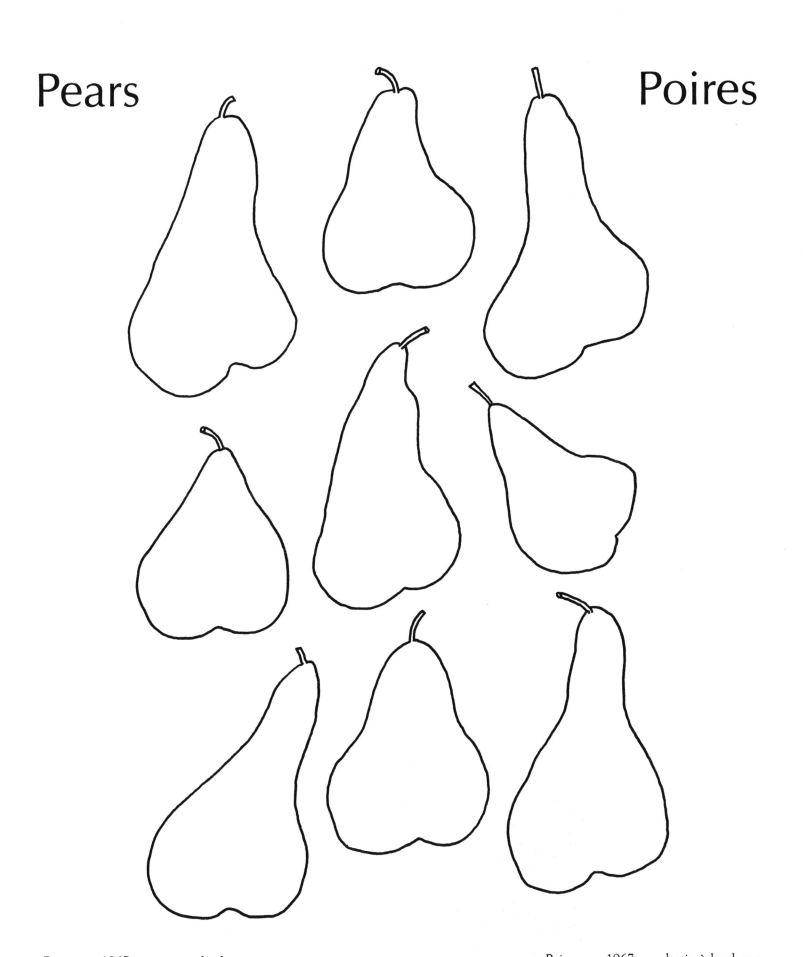

Pears   1967   pen and ink

Poires   1967   dessin à la plume

Pears   1960   pencil

Poires   1960   mine de plomb

Pears   1960-1962   pencil

Poires   1960-1962   mine de plomb

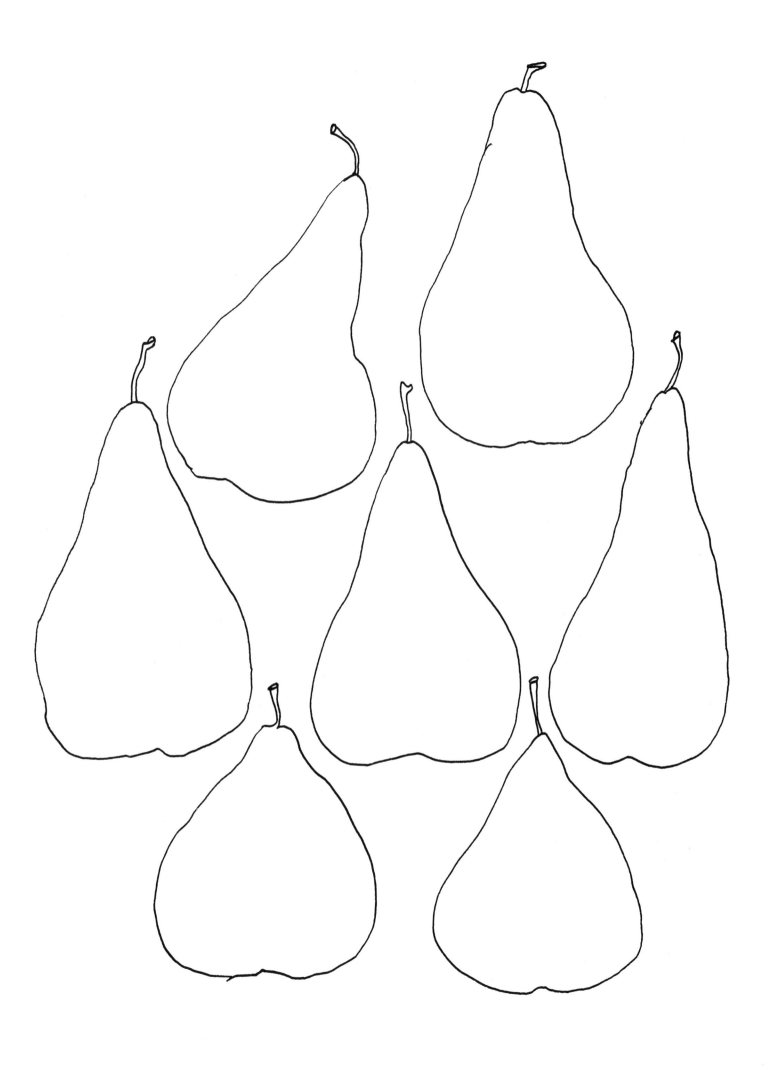

Pears   1963   pen and ink

Poires   1963   dessin à la plume

Pears   1964   colored pencil

Poires   1964   crayon de couleur

Undulatory drawings grew out of my experience as a film animator, in the following way. If, for example, I wished to make a single horizontal line undulate, I would make a series of separate drawings. On the first the line would be straight; on the second it would have a slight bend in it; on the third more than a bend; and so on. The principle being that each line is slightly and progressively different from the preceding. The rate of change varies at different parts of the line. The lines on my undulation drawings do exactly the same thing but on a page rather than in time. But I did not intend them to be looked at particularly in this way. It was only a device to arrive at a static composition.

Je me mis à pratiquer le dessin ondulatoire à partir du film d'animation. Voici comment cela s'est produit. Si je veux, par exemple, qu'une simple ligne horizontale ondule, je dois faire une série de dessins. Ligne droite sur le premier, courbe légère sur le deuxième, courbe plus accentuée sur le troisième et ainsi de suite, le principe consistant en une modification légère mais progressive à chaque dessin, le rythme de la progression pouvant varier ici ou là. Dans mes dessins ondulatoires, le même principe s'applique, mais sur le papier plutôt que dans le temps. Placés côte à côte sur une seule feuille, ils décrivent en quelque sorte la projection fixe de mouvements et donc, en un sens, du temps. Il n'était pas dans mon intention, cependant, de les faire voir sous cet aspect. Ce n'était pour moi qu'un moyen de pouvoir réaliser des compositions statiques.

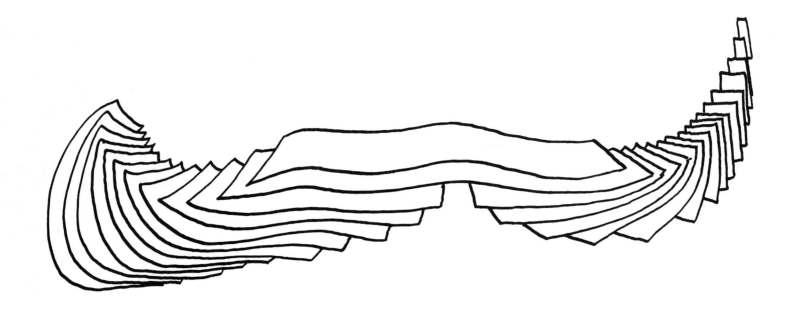

untitled   1963   pen and ink

sans titre   1963   dessin à la plume

12

Undulations

Ondulations

Doodled during the final mix of "Canon" 1964 pen and ink
I remember doing this when we were doing the final sound mix of the film "Canon" and we had a lot of sitting around to do.

Gribouillis pendant le mixage final de "Canon" 1964 dessin à la plume
Je me souviens que c'est à la période du mixage final du son pour le film "Canon" que je mis à griffonner au cours de ces longues séances assises.

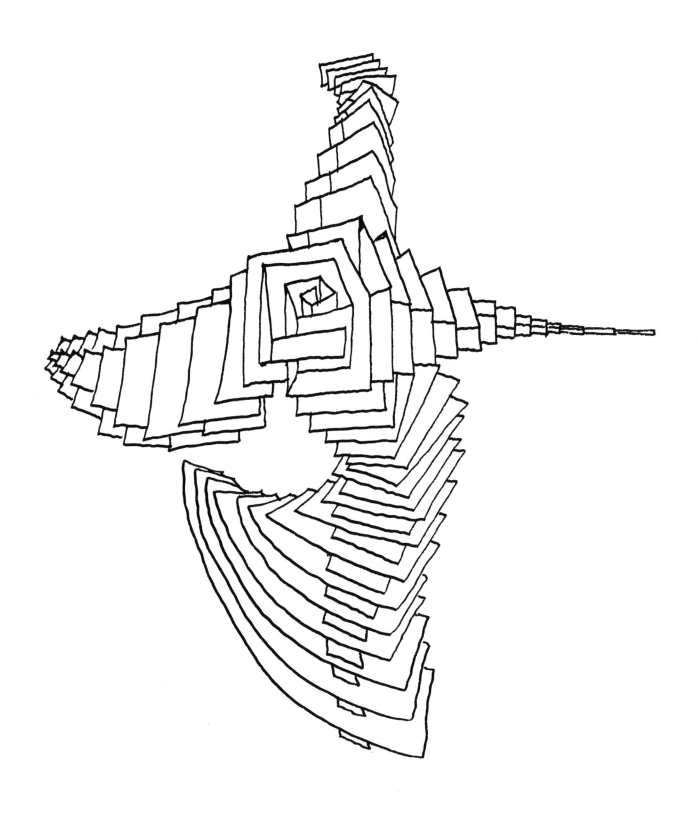

Metamorphic cross (double progression)   1965   pen
and ink

Croix métamorphique (en double
progression)   1965   dessin à la plume

30-second metamorphic doodles   undated   pen and ink   *Griffonnages de 30 secondes*   sans date   dessin à la plume

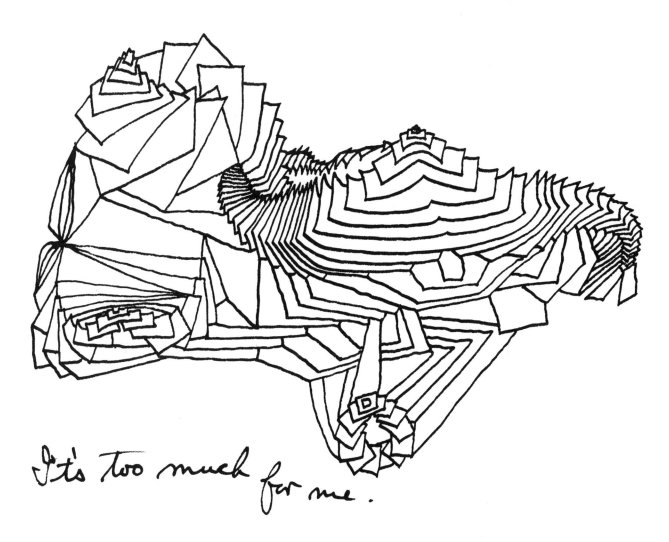

It's too much for me.

Congestion (It's too much for me)   1965   pen and ink   *Congestion (oh! la la!)*   1965   dessin à la plume

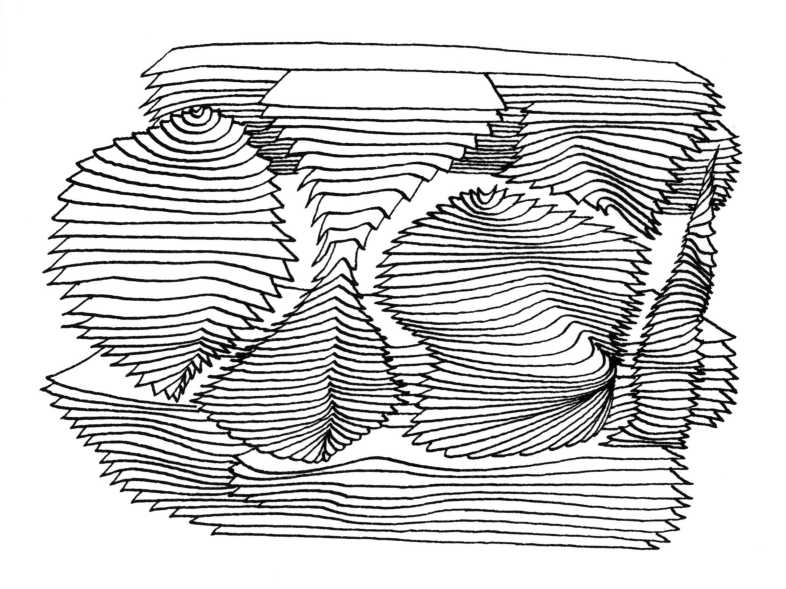

Mel.

12 April '65

untitled   1965   pen and ink
It was fun and a surprise sometimes, after I had been
drawing very close to the page, to move back and see the
form I'd made.

sans titre   1965   dessin à la plume
C'était amusant et parfois surprenant de regarder en me
reculant le motif que j'avais tracé de très près.

5 May 1965

6 May 1965

Circular undulation   1965   pen and ink
Circular undulations never worked out as well for me as a more rectilinear type did.

Ondulation circulaire   1965   dessin à la plume
Les ondulations circulaires n'ont jamais aussi bien donné, pour moi, que les ondulations de type plus rectiligne.

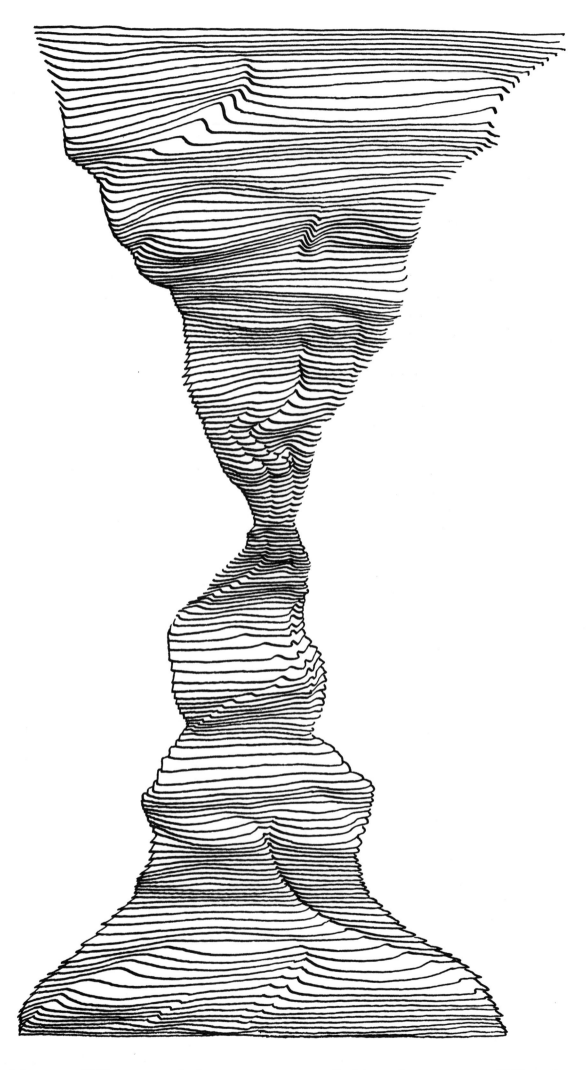

Pivot-type undulation   1965   pen and ink   *Ondulation de type pivot*   1965   dessin à la plume

Balancing undulation   undated   pen and ink   *Ondulation en équilibre*   sans date   dessin à la plume

Open-spaced undulation   undated   pen and ink

Ondulation en espace libre   sans date   dessin à la plume

Landscape near Annecy   1965   pen and ink   *Paysage près de Annecy*   1965   dessin à la plume

Open-spaced undulation   1966   pen and ink   *Ondulation en espace libre*   1966   dessin à la plume

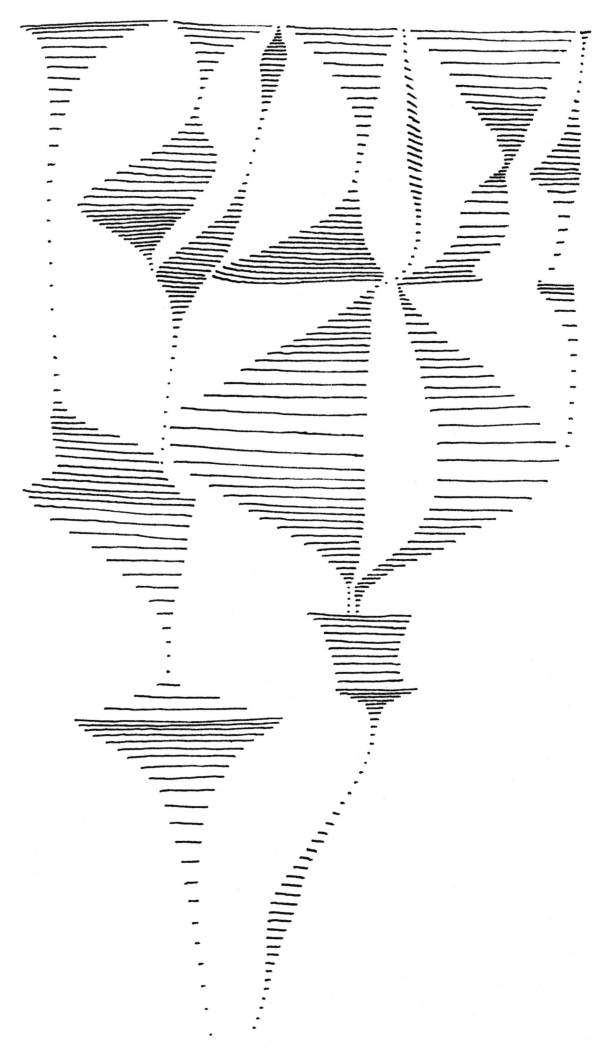

Open spaces undated pen and ink *Grands espaces* sans date dessin à la plume

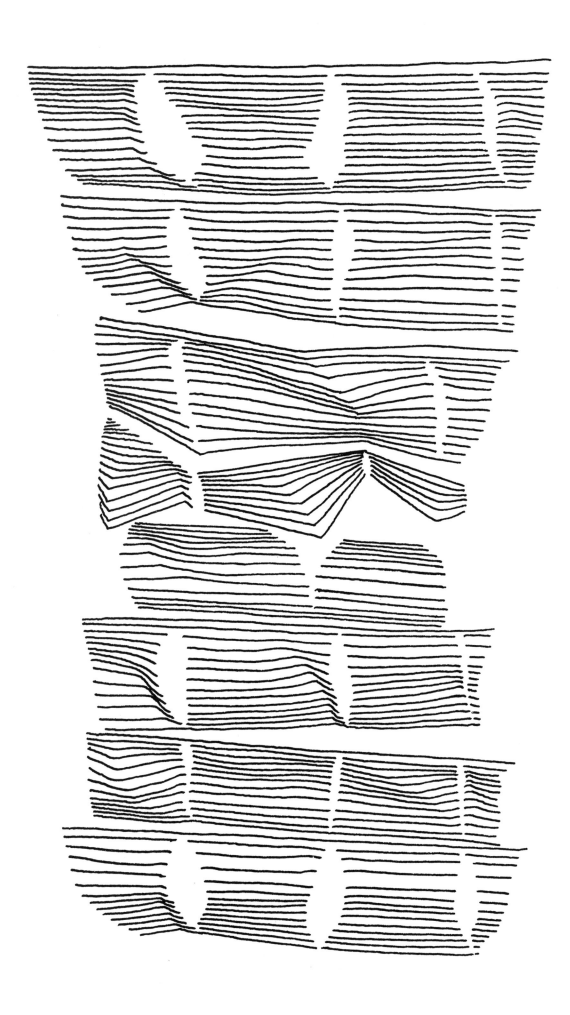

Lamination   1967   pen and ink

Lamination   1967   dessin à la plume

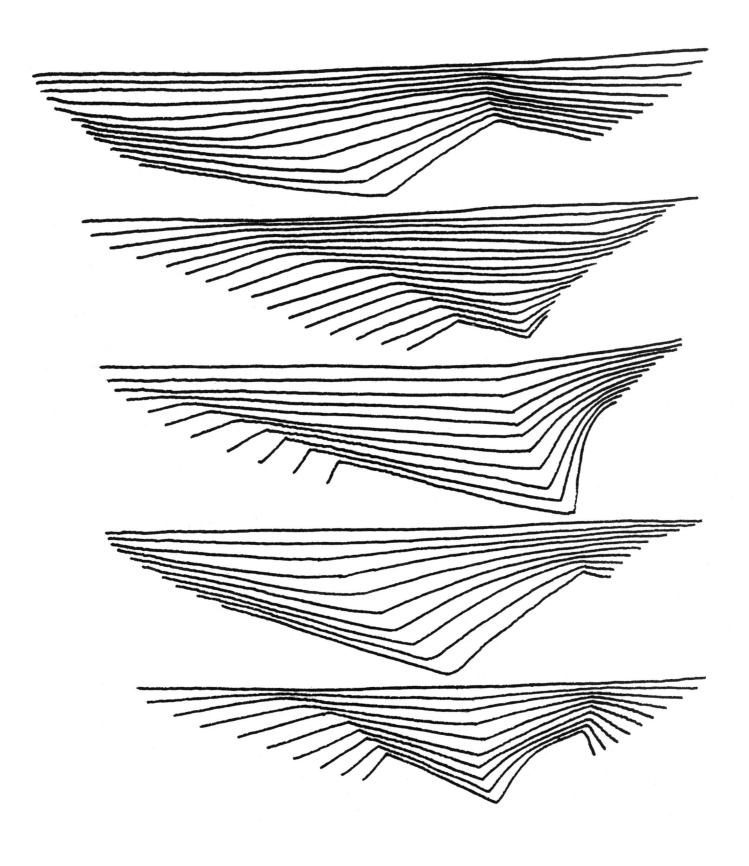

5 Jan 1967

N.

Flight   1967   pen and ink   Vol   1967   dessin à la plume

Triptych   1965   pen and ink   Triptyque   1965   dessin à la plume

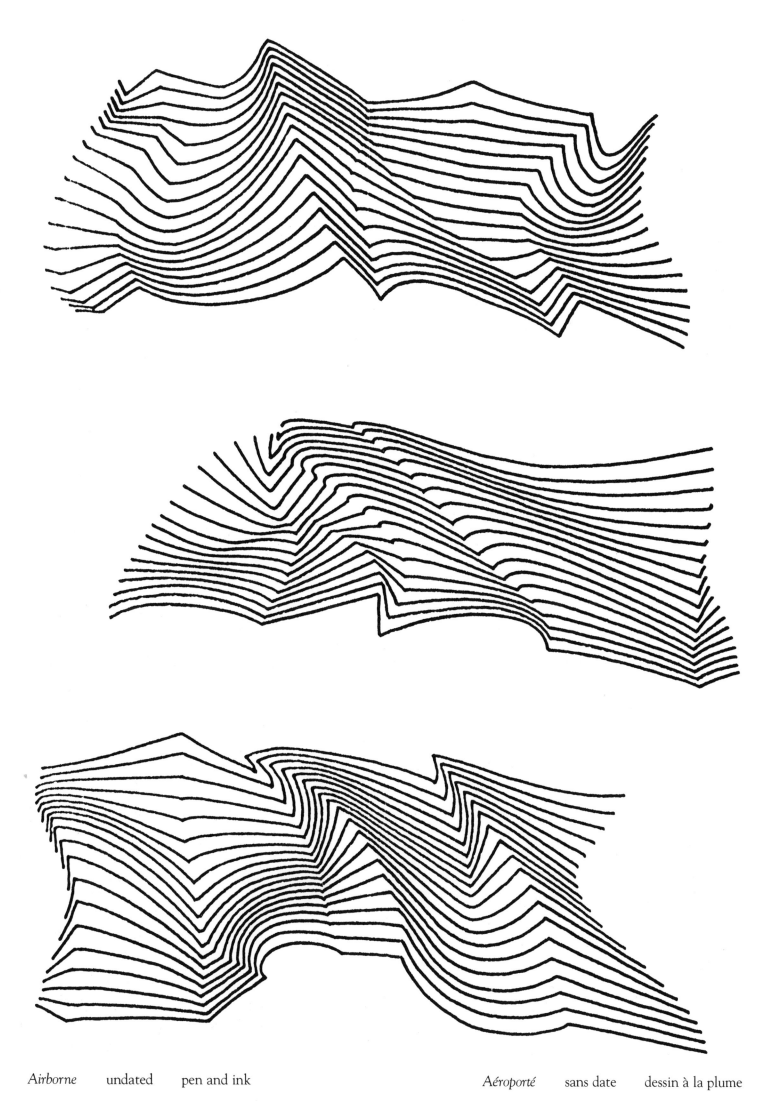

Airborne   undated   pen and ink   *Aéroporté*   sans date   dessin à la plume

Flow   1968   pen and ink

Flot   1968   dessin à la plume

Stress   1971   pen and ink   (The Graphic Guild)   *Tension*   1971   dessin à la plume   (La Guilde graphique)

Appendix

Annexe

untitled   1944   quill pen and india ink   sans titre   1944   plume d'oie et encre de chine

168

Other drawings

Autres dessins

1950   colored pencils

sans titre   1950   crayons de couleur

Anatomical drawings

Dessins d'anatomie

Heads and faces

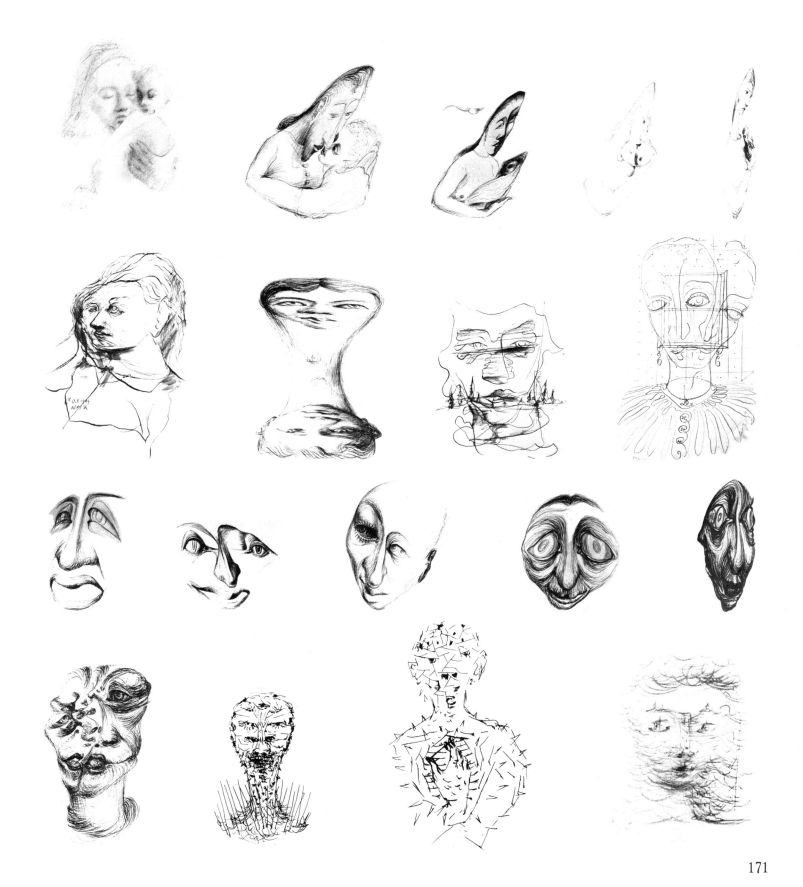

Music

Musique

THEME AND VARIATIONS:

A musical form which makes use of a principle theme upon which the structure of the composition is based. The variations consist in modifying a melody in its secondary elements, whether by substituting for each original note a group of shorter notes of equivalent value, or by altering the rhythm or time, or by changing the mode, key or harmony; but on the strict condition that the listener can always distinguish the original theme.

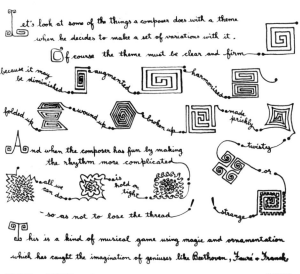

Let's look at some of the things a composer does with a theme when he decides to make a set of variations with it. Of course the theme must be clear and firm because it may be diminished, augmented, harmonised, folded up, wound up, broken up, made prickly, twisty, or strange. And when the composer has fun by making the rhythm more complicated — all we can do is hold on tight — so as not to lose the thread. This is a kind of musical game using magic and ornamentation which has caught the imagination of geniuses like Beethoven, Fauré & Franck.

Here is the dictionary definition.

RONDEAU: RONDO. One of the primitive types of musical structures & this form which appeared in the first half of the 13th century. It was first of all, a sort of "round-dance" or rondo and the rondeau was the dancing song which guided it. The rondeau is made up of a repeated refrain and several couplets. The melody of the refrain governs the complete rondeau since the 13th century. It has become a part of the symphony. The quartet and the sonata forms. The Italian form rondo has since prevailed and is a frequent form for the last movement of the sonata and the classical symphony.

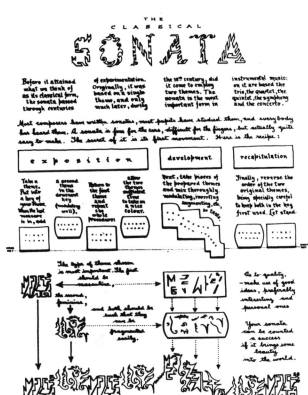

THE CLASSICAL SONATA

Before it attained what we think of as the classical form, the sonata passed through centuries of experimentation. Originally, it was based on a single theme, and only much later, during the 18th century, did it come to employ two themes. The sonata is the most important form in instrumental music; on it are based the trio, the quartet, the quintet, the symphony and the concerto.

Most composers have written sonatas, most pupils have studied them, and everybody has heard them. A sonata is fine for the ears, difficult for the fingers, but actually quite easy to make. The secret of it is its first movement. Here is the recipe:

exposition	development	recapitulation

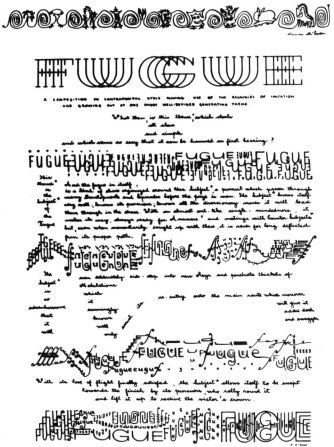

A composition in contrapuntal style making use of the resources of imitation and growing out of one short well-defined generating theme.

Wash drawings

Lavis

Fantasy

Fantaisie

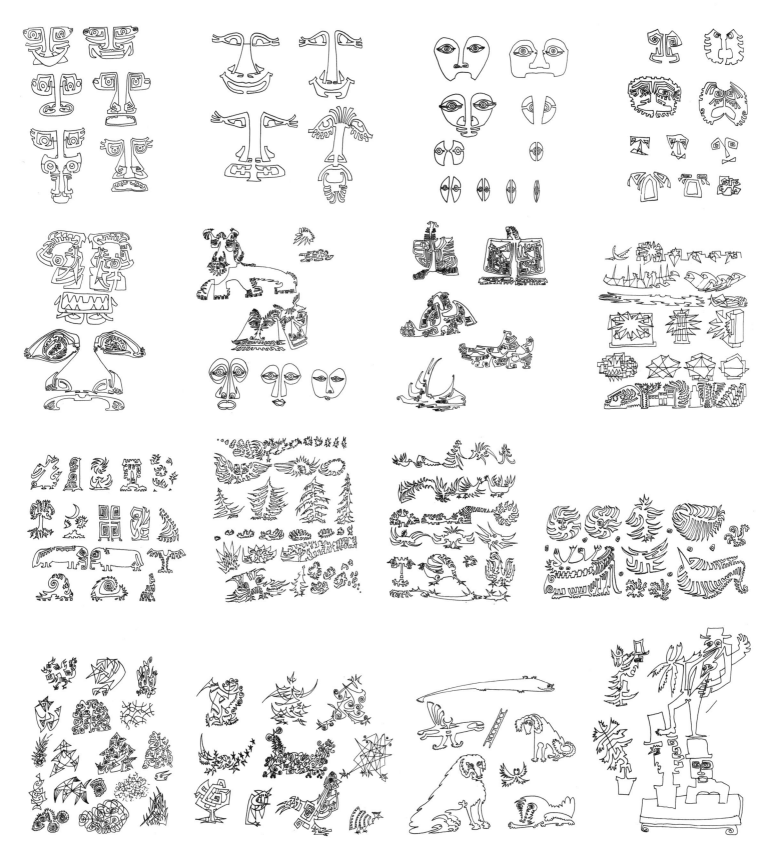

178

4.45am. DAWN LIGHT. 21 July 1963

Letters

Lettres

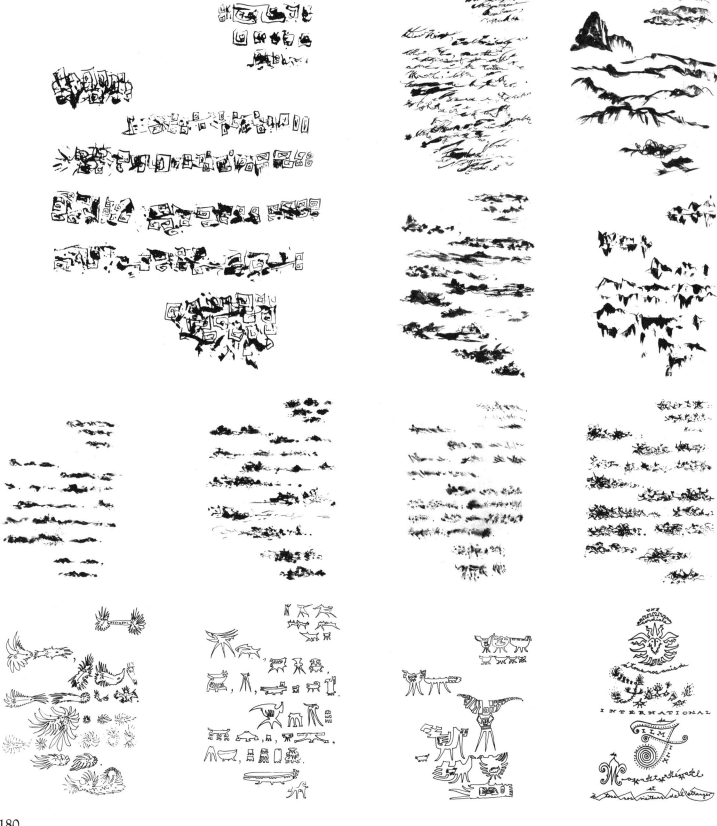

180

Undulations Ondulations

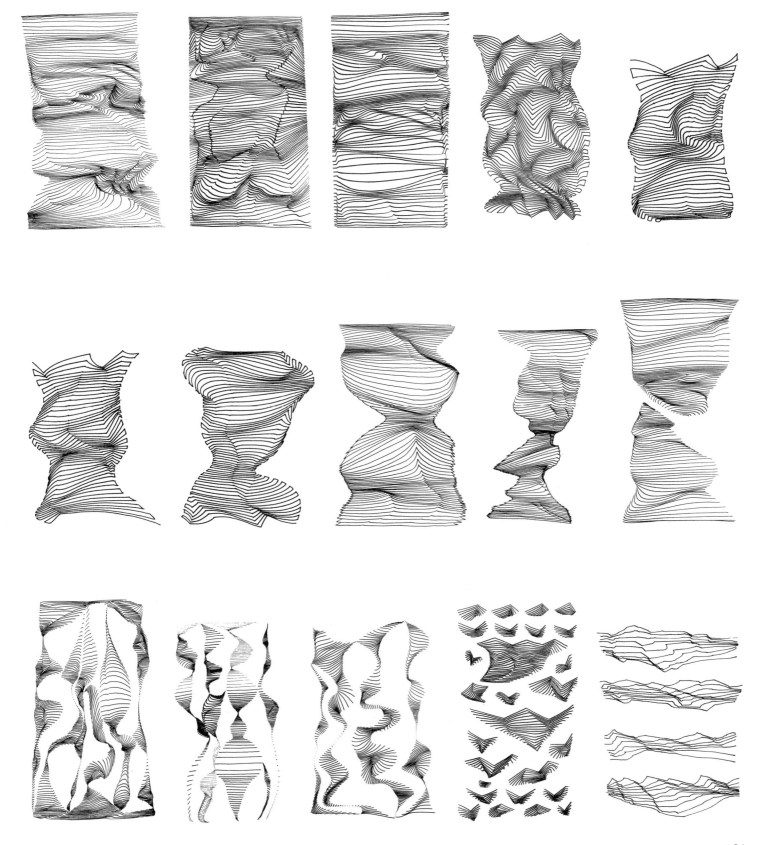

Bibliography

Bibliographie

Benayoun, Robert (1961) **Dessin animé après Walt Disney** Paris, Pauvert, p. 24-28, 92-108

Cutler, M. E. (1965) "Unique genius of Norman McLaren" **Canadian Art,** No. 22, May-June, p. 8-17

Elliott, Lawrence (1971) "Norman McLaren: Gentle Genius of the Screen" **Reader's Digest,** August

Glover, Guy (1970) "Nine Film Animators Speak," section by Norman McLaren **Arts Canada,** April

Jordan, William E. (1954) "Norman McLaren: His Career and Techniques" **Quarterly of Film, Radio, and Television,** VIII (1)

Martin, André (1958) i x i= . . . ou le cinéma de deux mains. **Cahiers du Cinéma,** No. 79, janvier, p. 5-19

Martin, André (1958) i x i= . . . ou le cinéma de deux mains. Portrait d'un aventurier. **Cahiers du Cinéma,** No. 80, février, p. 27-35

Martin, André (1958) i x i= . . . mystère d'un cinéma instrumental. II — Secrets de fabrication. **Cahiers du Cinéma,** No. 81, mars, p. 41-46

Martin, André (1958) i x i= . . . mystère d'un cinéma instrumental. III — On a touché au cinéma. **Cahiers du Cinéma,** No. 82, avril, p. 34-37

McDermot, Anne (1959) **Vie des arts,** #16, p. 18-25, automne, Montréal

McDermot, Anne (1955) Norman McLaren o della purezza nel cinema. **Bianco e Nero,** Numéro 1-2, Gennaio-Febrraio, p. 31-49

McLaren, Norman, with appendix by Chester Beachell (1951) "Stereographic animation" **SMPTE Journal,** Dec. p. 513-520

McWilliams, Don (1969) "Talking to a Great Film Artist — Norman McLaren" **McGill Reporter,** I (35), April 28

Morris, Peter, editor (1965) "The National Film Board of Canada: The War Years" **Canadian Film Archives, Canadian Filmography Series No. 3** Canadian Film Institute, Ottawa

National Film Board of Canada Film Catalogue (1975-1976)

"Norman McLaren" (1965) **Journées Internationales du Cinéma d'Animation Cinémathèque Canadienne,** Montréal

Séquences, (1975) Ed. Léo Bonneville, Vol. 18, Oct.

Warkentin, G. (1957) "Norman McLaren" **Tamarack Review,** automne, p. 42

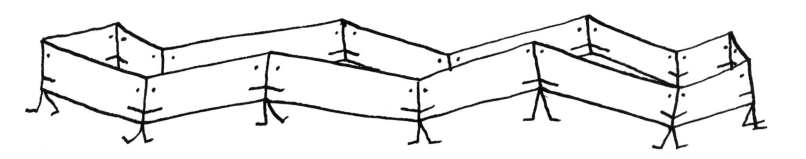

Filmography

Filmographie

(1914 Born)

Glasgow School of Art Period (1933-1936)

1933 (untitled) 35 mm, silent, 300 feet (a hand-painted abstraction made with colored dyes; the first attempt to draw directly on film, with Stewart McAllister)

1933 **Seven Till Five** bw, 16 mm, 10 min, silent (school activities from 7 am to 5 pm; a formalized documentary of a day's activity at the GSA)

1935 **Camera Makes Whoopee** bw, 16 mm, 15 min, silent (a school Christmas ball; conventional animation, models and frame-by-frame movement of objects, with trick-camera effects)

1935 **Colour Cocktail** Dufaycolor, 16 mm, 5 min, silent (live shooting, slow-motion, play of lights on colored paper; camera movements to be played with synchronous accompaniment on disc)

1935 (five untitled films) Dufaycolor, 16 mm, silent, total of 1000 feet (short advertising films for a local retail meat store; used in window display projections)

1936 **Hell Unlimited** bw, 16 mm, 15 min, silent (coproduced with Helen Biggar) (an antiwar film using both animations and real-object photography, with diagrams, animated maps, puppets, and live shots)

1936 Cameraman for **Defence of Madrid** directed by Ivor Montagu (a Spanish Civil War documentary)

General Post Office Film Unit, London Period (1937-1939)
1937 **Book Bargain** bw, 35 mm, 10 min, sound (a documentary on the printing of the London phone directory)

1937 **News for the Navy** bw, 35 mm, 10 min, sound (a documentary film)

1938 **Mony a Pickle** bw, 35 mm, 2 min, sound (a fantasy, publicizing the Post Office savings bank, in which furniture is animated by live photography to tell a story)

1938 **Love on the Wing** Dufaycolor, 35 mm, 5½ min, sound (a fantasy publicizing the new airmail service, made to the music of Jacques Ibert's "Divertissement"; hand-drawn cameraless technique used, plus photographic multiplane backgrounds)

Film Centre, London Period (1939)
1939 **The Obedient Flame** bw, 35 mm, 20 min, sound (a film on cooking gas made with animation and regular photography)

New York City Period (1939-1941)
1939 Directed a New Year's Greetings film for NBC

1939 *****Allegro** color, 35 mm, 2 min, sound (an abstraction with both picture and synthetic sound hand drawn frame by frame)

1939 *****Rumba** bw, 35 mm, 2½ min, sound only (a synthetic sound composition — no visuals — made by the cameraless method, drawing sound-forms directly on raw film)

(Naissance: 1914)

École des Beaux-Arts de Glasgow (1933-36)
1933 (sans titre) 35mm, sans paroles, 300 pieds (abstraction peinte à la main, teintures de couleur; première tentative de dessin directement sur la pellicule) Collaborateur: Stewart McAllister

1933 **Seven Till Five** noir et blanc, 16mm, 10 minutes, muet (activités dans une école de 7h à 17h; documentaire conventionnel d'une journée à l'École des Beaux-Arts de Glasgow)

1935 **Camera Makes Whoopee** noir et blanc, 16mm, 15 minutes, muet (bal de Noël dans une école; animation traditionnelle, technique image par image et effets spéciaux)

1935 **Colour Cocktail** Dufaycolor, 16mm, 5 minutes (filmé en direct, ralenti, jeux de lumière sur papier de couleur; mouvements de caméra devant être synchronisés avec accompagnement sur disque)

(5 films sans titre) Dufaycolor, 16mm, muet, 1000 pieds (courts films publicitaires pour une boucherie locale destinés à être projetés dans la vitrine)

1936 **Hell Unlimited** noir et blanc, 16mm, 15 minutes, muet (co-produit avec Helen Biggar) (film contre la guerre combinant animation et photographies d'objets, ainsi que des diagrammes, des cartes animées, des marionnettes et du tournage en direct)

1936 Cameraman du film "Defence of Madrid" réalisé par Ivor Montagu (documentaire sur la guerre civile d'Espagne)

General Post Office, Section du Film, Londres (1937-39)
1937 **Book Bargain** noir et blanc, 35mm, 10 minutes sonore (documentaire sur l'impression de l'annuaire téléphonique de Londres) (expériences sur le son synthétique) non utilisé (première tentative de dessin à la plume, directement sur la pellicule produisant un registre étendu de sons semi-musicaux, principalement des sons de percussion)

1937 **News for the Navy** noir et blanc, 35mm, 10 minutes, sonore (film documentaire)

1938 **Mony a Pickle** noir et blanc, 35mm, 2 minutes, sonore (une fantaisie destinée à la publicité du Post Office Savings Bank, où des photos de meubles sont animées pour raconter une histoire)

1938 **Love on the Wing** Dufaycolor, 35mm, 5 minutes 30 secondes, sonore (une fantaisie destinée à la publicité du nouveau service postal aérien, musique d'après le "Divertissement" de Jacques Ibert, images dessinées directement sur la pellicule avec fonds photographiques à plans multiples)

Film Centre, Londres (1939)
1939 **The Obedient Flame** noir et blanc, 35mm, 20 minutes, sonore (film sur la cuisson au gaz; animation et photographie)

New York (1939-41)
1939 Réalisé pour la chaîne de télévision: NBC offrant ses

1939 *Stars and Stripes color, 35 mm, 3 min, sound (a fantasy on the American flag in which "stars" and "stripes" perform activities to a sprightly march tune; frame by frame hand-drawn pictures with recorded soundtrack)

1940 *Dots color, 35 mm, 2½ min, sound

1940 Loops color, 35 mm, 3 min, sound

1940 *Boogie-Doodle color, 35 mm, 3½ min, sound (an abstraction, hand drawn directly on film, with boogie-woogie music played by Albert Ammons)

1940 Script and lyric writing for unidentified motion pictures for Carvelle Films, Inc., New York

1940 Spook Sport color, 35 mm, 9 min, sound (coproduced with Mary Ellen Bute) (a semiabstract visualization to Saint-Saëns "La danse macabre")

National Film Board of Canada Period (1941-Present)
1941 Mail Early for Christmas color, 35 mm, 2 min, sound (a fantasy dance of the Christmas mail, set to Benny Goodman's "Jingle Bells"; frame by frame hand drawing with multiplane traveling backgrounds)

1941 V for Victory Warnercolor, 35 mm, 2 min, sound (a short film set to a Sousa military march publicizing war savings; cameraless animation)

1942 Hen Hop Warnercolor, 35 mm, 3 min, sound (a rather fanciful hen dances to barn-dance music to incite rural populations to buy war bonds; cameraless animation)

1942 Five for Four Vitacolor, 35 mm, 4 min, sound (a film publicizing war savings set to the rhythms of "Pintop's Boogie" by Albert Ammons; cameraless animation)

1943 Dollar Dance Vitacolor, 35 mm, 5½ min, sound (a film on the dangers of inflation; music by Louis Applebaum and lyrics by Norman McLaren and Guy Glover; frame by frame hand-drawn pictures with moving backgrounds)

Animation Department at the NFB set up by McLaren

1944 General Supervisor of the "Chants populaires" series (CP series)

1944 Keep Your Mouth Shut bw, 35 mm, 3 min, sound (a film publicizing a campaign against war gossip, with live shooting and animation of objects; assisted by George Dunning)

1945 C'est l'aviron bw, 35 mm, 3 min, sound (CP series) (a film of white gouache drawings on black, using the staggered overlapping mix technique to achieve a moving multiplane effect)

voeux à l'occasion du Nouvel An

1939 *Allegro couleur, 35mm, 2 minutes, sonore (abstraction; images et son synthétique tracés à la main selon la technique image par image)

1939 *Rumba noir et blanc, 2 minutes 30 secondes, son seulement (composition de sons synthétiques reproduits à la main directement sur la pellicule)

1939 *Stars and Stripes couleur, 35mm, 3 minutes, sonore (fantaisie sur le drapeau américain; étoiles et bandes exécutent des acrobaties au son d'une musique martiale; technique image par image et trame sonore enregistrée)

1940 *Dots couleur, 35mm, 2 minutes 30 secondes, sonore

1940 Loops couleur, 35mm, 3 minutes, sonore

1940 *Boogie-Doodle couleur, 35mm, 3 minutes 30 secondes, sonore (abstraction directement dessinée sur la pellicule sur une musique de boogie-wogie jouée par Albert Ammons) Paroles et musique commandées par Carvelle Films, Inc., New York, pour un film non identifié

1940 Spook Sport couleur, 35mm, 9 minutes, sonore (produit par Mary Ellen Bute), animation Norman McLaren (interprétation semi-abstraite de "La danse macabre" de Saint-Saëns)

Office national du film (1941 à nos jours)

1941 Mail Early for Christmas couleur, 35mm, 2 minutes, sonore (Une fantaisie dansée sur l'air de "Jingle Bells", de Benny Goodman à l'occasion du courrier de Noël; technique image par image)

1941 V for Victory Warnercolor, 35mm, 2 minutes, sonore (un petit film sur une musique militaire de Souza vantant l'épargne en temps de guerre; animation sans caméra)

1942 Hen Hop Warnercolor, 35mm, 3 minutes, sonore (fantaisie sans paroles, dessin animé de McLaren incitant la population rurale à l'acquisition d'obligations de la victoire; animation sans caméra)

1942 Five for Four Vitacolor, 35mm, 4 minutes, sonore (film d'animation sans caméra encourageant l'achat d'obligations de la victoire au rythme de "Pintop's Boogie" par Albert Ammons)

1943 Dollar Dance Vitacolor, 35mm, 5 minutes 30 secondes, sonore (film sur les dangers de l'inflation, musique de Louis Applebaum et couplets de Norman McLaren et Guy Glover; technique image par image sur fonds animés)

Mise sur pied par Norman McLaren du département d'animation

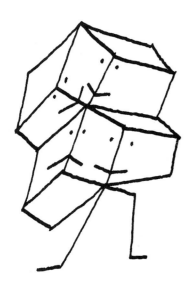

1946 **Là-haut sur ces montagnes** bw, 35 mm, 3 min, sound (CP series) (an illustration of the folk song made with animation camera and pastel method)

1946 **A Little Phantasy on a 19th Century Painting** bw, 35 mm, 3½ min, sound (a film based on the painting "Isle of the Dead" by Arnold Boecklin; produced by the pastel method)

1946 **Hoppity Pop** color, 35 mm, 2½ min, sound (three decorative motifs to barrel-organ music, with frame by frame hand-drawn pictures)

1947 **Fiddle-De-Dee** color, 35 mm, 3½ min, sound (cameraless abstraction, made largely without reference to the frame divisions in the film, set to a Gatineau Valley old-time fiddler's spirited rendition of "Listen to the Mocking Bird")

1947 **La poulette grise** Kodachrome, 16 mm, 5½ min, sound (CP series) (illustration of Anna Malenfant's rendition of the folk song, with pastel method animation)

1949 **Begone Dull Care** color, 35 mm, 7½ min, sound (codirected with Evelyn Lambart) (similar to "Fiddle-De-Dee," set to music played by the Oscar Peterson jazz trio)

Goes to China to work on a UNESCO experiment in fundamental education and trains many Chinese students in the art of simple animation techniques

1950 **Pen Point Percussion** bw, 35 mm, 7 min, sound (a documentary showing McLaren's technique of hand-drawn sound on film; designed as an introduction to "Dots" and "Loops")

1951 **Around is Around** English Technicolor, 35 mm, 10 min, sound (an experimental 3-D film made for the Festival of Britain; a coproduction of the NFB and the British Film Institute) (abstract stereoscopic animation using cathode-ray oscillograph to generate mobile patterns; assisted by Evelyn Lambart; music by Louis Applebaum)

1951 **Now is the Time** English Technicolor, 35 mm, 3 min, sound (an experimental 3-D film made for the festival of Britain; a coproduction of the NFB and the British Film Institute) (paper cutouts and direct drawing on film, with stereoscopic animation and stereophonic sound)

1952 **A Phantasy** Kodachrome, 16 mm, 7 min, sound (begun in 1948) (a semiabstract, semisurrealist essay made by the pastel method and using some cutouts; music for saxophones and synthetic sound by Maurice Blackburn)

1952 **Two Bagatelles** Kodachrome, 16 mm, 2½ min, sound (two short films in which the principles of animation normally

à l'Office national du film

1944 Supervision de la série "Chants populaires"

1944 **Keep Your Mouth Shut** noir et blanc, 35mm, 3 minutes, sonore (film sur les commérages en temps de guerre, tournage en direct et animation d'objets; assistant George Dunning)

1945 **C'est l'aviron** noir et blanc, 35mm, 3 minutes, sonore (dessins à la gouache blanche sur fond noir et produisant par décalage un effet de plans multiples en mouvement)

1945 **Là-haut sur ces montagnes** noir et blanc, 35mm, 3 minutes, sonore (illustration d'un chant populaire à l'aide de pastels animés)

1946 **A Little Phantasy on a 19th Century Painting** 35mm, 3 minutes 30 secondes, sonore (film basé sur le tableau "Isle of the Dead" d'Arnold Boecklin et exécuté au moyen de pastels animés)

1946 **Hoppity Pop** couleur, 35mm, 2 minutes 30 secondes, sonore (des formes multicolores suivent pas à pas le rythme qu'égrène un orgue de barbarie; dessiné directement sur la pellicule image par image)

1947 **Fiddle-De-Dee** couleur, 35mm, 3 minutes 30 secondes, sonore (abstraction sans caméra réglée sur l'exécution pleine d'entrain de "Listen to the Mocking Bird" par un violoneux de la vallée de la Gatineau)

1947 **La poulette grise** Kodachrome, 16mm, 5 minutes 30 secondes, sonore (illustration de la chanson interprétée par Anna Malenfant, animation au pastel)

1949 **Begone Dull Care** couleur, 35mm, 7 minutes 30 secondes, sonore (réalisation conjointe avec Evelyn Lambart) (même technique que "Fiddle-De-Dee"; musique par le trio de jazz Oscar Peterson)

McLaren est délégué en Chine par l'UNESCO; enseigne à des étudiants chinois les techniques de base d'animation sans caméra et autres techniques audio-visuelles

1950 **Pen Point Percussion** noir et blanc, 35mm, 7 minutes, sonore (documentaire illustrant la technique McLaren du son synthétique dessiné sur film; servira de prologue à "Dots" et "Loops")

1951 **Around is Around** Technicolor, production ONF et British Film Institute, 35mm, 10 minutes, sonore (film expérimental tridimensionnel à l'occasion du Festival of Britain) (abstraction animée en stéréoscopie par oscillographe à rayon cathodique engendrant des motifs animés; Evelyn Lambart, assistante); musique: Louis Applebaum

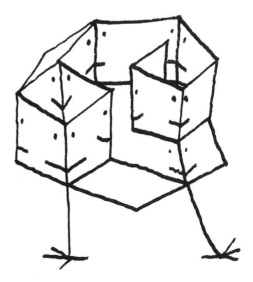

used to put drawings into motion are used to animate live actors, i.e. frame-by-frame animation of human beings)

1952 **Neighbours** Kodachrome, 16 mm, 8 min, sound (this film, using frame by frame animation of humans, is a simple parable about two people who come to blows over the possession of a flower)

1953 Leaves for India to participate in another UNESCO project

1954 **Blinkity Blank** color, 35 mm, 6 min, sound (image flashes of fantastic animals mating and fighting one another in intermittent animation; scratched at intervals on blank 35 mm film, with instrumental music of Maurice Blackburn supplemented by McLaren's drawn sounds)

1956 **Rythmetic** color, 35 mm, 8½ min, sound (cutouts of numbers given life and motion to prompt interest in classrooms and literacy programs; assisted by Evelyn Lambart)

1957 **A Chairy Tale** bw, 35 mm, 9½ min, sound (codirected with Claude Jutra) (live actor animation showing pas de deux of man and chair, Eastern music on Indian instruments by Ravi Shankar)

1958 **Le Merle** color, 35 mm, 4 min, sound (paper strips animated to illustrate actions of the blackbird in the folk song; assisted by Evelyn Lambart, music by Maurice Blackburn)

1959 **Serenal** color, 16 mm, 3 min, sound (semiabstract illustration of a West Indies drumband tune, etched directly on 16 mm film with a vibra drill and colored, largely without reference to the frame divisions of the film)

1959 **Short and Suite** color, 35 mm, 5 min, sound (abstract cameraless animation, in the manner of "Fiddle-De-Dee," etched on film with a vibra drill; music is an ensemble of jazz by Eldon Rathburn)

1959 **Mail Early for Christmas** color, 35 mm, 30 sec, sound (another version of an earlier film this time with cameraless animation etched on film with a vibra drill)

Makes credit titles for the television show, "The Wonderful World of Jack Paar"

1960 **Lines Vertical** color, 35 mm, 5½ min, sound (experiment in pure design by Norman McLaren and Evelyn Lambart — lines, ruled directly on the film, move against a background of changing colors in response to music)

1960 **Opening Speech** bw, 35 mm, 7 min, sound (originally made for the official opening of the Montreal Film Festival; McLaren attempts with absolutely no success to deliver a speech

1951 **Now is the Time** Technicolor, production ONF et British Film Institute, 35mm, 3 minutes, sonore (film expérimental tridimensionnel à l'occasion du Festival of Britain) (papier découpé et dessins exécutés directement sur la pellicule, animation en stéréoscopie et son en stéréophonie)

1952 **A Phantasy** Kodachrome, 16mm, 7 minutes, sonore (commencé en 1948) (variations mi-abstraites, mi-surréalistes; pastels animés et papier découpé; musique de Maurice Blackburn pour saxophones et son synthétique)

1952 **Two Bagatelles** Kodachrome, 16mm, 2 minutes 30 secondes, sonore, interprétation: Grant Munro (valse et marche rapide d'un personnage aux mouvements irrationnels, animation d'un personnage vivant)

1952 **Les Voisins** Kodachrome, 16mm, 8 minutes, sonore (parabole toute simple sur deux voisins qui se disputent jusqu'à en venir aux coups la possession d'une fleur) technique image par image

1953 McLaren part pour les Indes où il prend part à l'exécution d'un programme d'instruction dû à l'initiative de l'UNESCO et du Gouvernement indien

1954 **Blinkity Blank** couleur, 35mm, 5 minutes, sonore (apparitions éclairs d'animaux fantastiques s'accouplant ou se combattant, animation basée sur la persistance retinienne, musique instrumentale de Maurice Blackburn)

1956 **Rythmetic** couleur, 35mm, 8 minutes 30 secondes, sonore (petit cours élémentaire d'arithmétique, animation de chiffres découpés) collaboration: Evelyn Lambart

1957 **Il était une chaise** noir et blanc, 35mm, 9 minutes 30 secondes, sonore (co-réalisateur: Claude Jutra) (animation avec acteur réel; pas de deux du personnage et de la chaise; musique: Ravi Shankar)

1958 **Le Merle** couleur, 35mm, 4 minutes, sonore (illustration de la chanson interprétée par le Trio Lyrique) papier découpé, collaboration: Evelyn Lambart, musique: Maurice Blackburn

1959 **Serenal** couleur, 16mm, 3 minutes, sonore (variations abstraites sur une musique populaire des Antilles, gravure au moyen d'une foreuse pneumatique miniature et peinture sur pellicule non cadrée)

1959 **Short and Suite** couleur, 35mm, 5 minutes, sonore (abstraction animée sans caméra, style "Fiddle-De-Dee", gravée sur pellicule, musique de jazz, direction: Eldon Rathburn)

1959 **Mail Early for Christmas** couleur, 35mm, 30 secondes, sonore (autre version d'un film antérieur avec, cette fois, animation sans caméra, dessin sur pellicule)

via a recalcitrant microphone)

1961 **New York Lightboard — Welcome to Canada** bw, 35 mm, 8 min, silent (publicizing film for the Canadian Tourist Bureau) (cameraless animation combined with frame by frame animation of individual drawings on small pieces of paper and with cutout letters; the film was designed for use in a special advertising lightboard on Times Square in New York City)

1962 **Lines Horizontal** color, 35 mm, 5½ min, sound, assisted by Evelyn Lambart (abstract variation based on a single line; made by optically turning each frame of "Lines Vertical" by ninety degrees; music by Pete Seeger)

1962 **Christmas Cracker** color, 35 mm, 9 min, sound (animation of a human being)

1964 **Canon** color, 35 mm, 10 min, sound (Norman McLaren and Grant Munro demonstrate by animation and live action how the musical canon is constructed; with cubes, cutout silhouettes, human beings, and one cat, music by Eldon Rathburn)

1965 **Mosaic** bw and color, 35 mm, 5½ min, sound, assisted by Evelyn Lambart ("op" art in film; a single tiny square divides into many segments, eventually forming a colorful mosaic; made by combining parts of "Lines — Vertical and Horizontal" to produce a ballet of points)

1967 **Pas de deux** bw, 35 mm, 13½ min, sound (a film of two ballet dancers, Margaret Mercier and Vincent Warren; by exposing the frame as many as ten times, a multiple image of the single dancer and her partner is created)

1969 **Spheres** color, 35 mm, 7½ min, sound (piano Glenn Gould)

1971 **Synchromy** color, 35 mm, 7½ min, sound

1972 **Ballet Adagio** color, 35 mm, 10 minutes, sound (David and Anne-Marie Holmes — Pas de deux in slow motion)

Made for the Guggenheim Museum

Réalisation du générique pour l'émission télévisée "The Wonderful World of Jack Paar"

1960 **Lignes verticales** couleur, 35mm, 5 minutes 30 secondes, sonore (variations abstraites à partir d'une ligne) collaboration: Evelyn Lambart, musique: Maurice Blackburn

1960 **Discours de bienvenue de Norman McLaren** noir et blanc, 35mm, 7 minutes, sonore (conçu pour l'ouverture officielle du Festival du film de Montréal; le film montre McLaren lui-même essayant vainement de prononcer un discours derrière un micro rebelle)

1961 **New York Lightboard — Welcome to Canada** noir et blanc, 35mm, 8 minutes, muet, collaboration: Ron Tunis et Kaj Pindal (film publicitaire pour l'Office national du tourisme) (animation sans caméra combinée avec animation de papier et de lettres découpées) Film conçu pour être projeté sur un panneau publicitaire lumineux dans Times Square, New York

1962 **Lignes horizontales** couleur, 35mm, 5 minutes 30 secondes, sonore, collaboration: Evelyn Lambart (variations abstraites à partir d'une seule ligne produite en faisant tourner de 90 degrés chaque cadrage de "Lignes verticales"; musique de Pete Seeger)

1962 **Caprice de Noël** couleur, 35mm, 9 minutes, sonore

1964 **Canon** couleur, 35mm, 10 minutes, sonore (Norman McLaren et Grant Munro illustrent la structure d'un canon musical avec des cubes, des silhouettes découpées, des personnages et un chat) Musique: Eldon Rathburn

1965 **Mosaïque** noir et blanc, et couleur, 35mm, 5 minutes 30 secondes, sonore (art "op" appliqué au film; gravure sur pellicule cadrée, mise en application de la persistance rétinienne) Collaboration: Evelyn Lambart

1967 **Pas de deux** 35mm, noir et blanc, 13 minutes 30 secondes, sonore, Margaret Mercier et Vincent Warren, deux étoiles des Grands Ballets Canadiens évoluent sur un Pas de deux. L'exposition d'un plan jusqu'à dix fois engendre une image multiple du danseur et de sa partenaire

1969 **Sphères** couleur, 35mm, 7 minutes 30 secondes, sonore (commencé en 1948)

1971 **Synchromie** couleur, 35mm, 7 minutes 30 secondes, sonore

1972 **Ballet Adagio** couleur, 35mm, 10 minutes, sonore (David et Anne-Marie Holmes évoluent en un Pas de deux sur l'Adagio d'Albinoni. Le film tourné au ralenti souligne la maîtrise des danseurs.)

Films réalisés pour le Musée Guggenheim

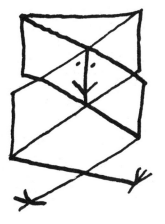

Awards

1942 **Hen Hop** Special Award, Brussels Film Festival, 1949-50

1946 **A Little Phantasy on a 19th Century Painting** Chamber of Commerce of Salerno Cup, Best Avant-Garde Film, Documentary Film Festival, Salerno, Italy, 1950-51

1947 **Fiddle-De-Dee** Special Award, Brussels Film Festival, 1949-50; Gulf of Salerno Trophy (First.Award), Documentary Film Festival, Salerno, 1950-51; Honor Certificate for Film Production in General, International Review of Specialized Cinematography, Rome 1955-56; Diploma of Honor, International Review of Specialized Cinematography, Rome, 1956-57

1948 **Dots/Points** Special Award, Canadian Film Awards, Toronto, 1948-49; Honorable Mention, Miscellaneous Film Section, Documentary Film Festival, Salerno, 1950-51; Diploma of Honor, International Review of Specialized Cinematography, Rome 1957-58

1948 **Loops/Boucles** Special Award, Canadian Film Awards, Toronto, 1948-49; Honorable Mention, Miscellaneous Films Section, Documentary Film Festival, Salerno, 1950-51; Honor Certificate for Film Production in General, Review of Specialized Cinematography, Rome, 1955-56

1950 **Begone Dull Care/Caprice en couleurs** Special Award, Canadian Film Awards, Toronto, 1949-50; Honorable Mention, Miscellaneous Film Section, Documentary Film Festival, Salerno, 1950-51; First Prize, Art Films Category, International Film Festival, Venice, 1950-51; Best Experimental Film, American Federation of Art and Film, Advisory Center Film Festival, Woodstock, N. Y., 1951-52; Silver Medal, Documentary Short Film Category, Berlin International Film Festival, 1951-52; First Award, Experimental Section, International Film Festival, Durban, South Africa, 1954-55

1950 **Pen Point Percussion/A la pointe de la plume** Honorable Mention, Experimental Films Category, Venice International Film Festival

1952 **A Phantasy** Special Award, Non-theatrical Class, Canadian Film Awards, Toronto, 1952-53; Second Prize, Experimental Films Category, Venice International Film Festival, 1952-53; First Award, Arts Section, Boston Film Festival, Boston, Mass., 1953-54

1952 **Neighbours/Voisins** Academy Award, Best Documentary Short Subject, Hollywood, Calif., 1952-53; Special Award, Non-theatrical Class, Canadian Film Awards, Toronto, 1952-53; Award of Merit, Adult Education Section, Boston Film Festival, 1953-54; Gulf of Salerno Grand Trophy, Documentary Film Festival, Salerno, 1954-55; Third Award, Sociological Category, International Documentary Film Festival, Yorkton, Saskatchewan, 1954-55; Honor Certificate for Film Production in General, International Review of Specialized Cinematography, Rome, 1955-56; Diploma of Honor, International Review of Specialized Cinematography, Rome, 1957-58

1954 **Blinkity Blank** Silver Bear, Berlin International Film Festival, 1955-56; Grand Prix (Palme d'or) International Film Festival, Cannes, France, 1955-56; Certificate of Merit, Durban International Film Festival, 1955-56; Diploma of Merit, International Film Festival, Edinburgh, Scotland, 1955-56; First Prize, Best Animated Film, British Academy Awards, London, England, 1955-56; Fourth Prize, "Internation Prize," Paris, France, 1955-56; Certificate of Merit, International Documentary Film Festival, Capetown, South Africa, 1956-57; First Honorable Mention, Experimental Films Category, International Festival of Documentary and Experimental Films Montevideo, Uruguay, 1956-57; Selected for Screening, International Art Film Festival, New York, 1957-58; Diploma of Honor, International Review of Specialized Cinematography, Rome, 1957-58

1956 **Rythmetic** Silver Bear, Short Films Category, Berlin International Film Festival, 1956-57; Purchase (First) Prize, Festival of Contemporary Arts, Chicago, 1956-57; Certificate of Merit, Durban International Film Festival, 1956-57; Diploma of Merit, Edinburgh Film Festival, 1956-57; Certificate of Merit, International Film Festival, Johannesburg, South Africa, 1956-57; Nominated for Best Animated Film Award, British Film Academy, London, 1956-57; Silver Reel Award, Avant-Garde and Experimental Category, Golden Reel Film Festival, New York, 1957-58; First Prize, Abstract Films, International Film Festival, Rapallo, Italy, 1957-58; Diploma of Honor, International Review of Specialized Cinematography, Rome, 1957-58

1957 **A Chairy Tale/Il était une chaise** Nominated for Best Short Subject, Academy of Motion Picture Arts and Science, Hollywood, 1957-58; Special award for "work lying outside the feature and documentary fields," British Film Academy, London, 1957-58; First Prize, Experimental and Avant-Garde Category, International Exhibition of Documentary and Short Films, Venice, 1957-58; Second Prize, Experimental Film Category, Rapallo Film Festival; 1958-59; Award of Merit, Non-theatrical, Canadian Film Awards, Toronto, 1958-59

1958 **Le Merle** First Prize for Best Use of Color, World Film Festival, Brussels, 1958-59; Diploma of Honor, Film Festival, Locarno, Switzerland, 1958-59; Special Mention, Spanish, American and Philippines Film Festival, Bilbao, Spain, 1959-60; Mention, International Festival of Documentary and Experimental Film, Montevideo, Uruguay, 1960-61; Blue Ribbon Award, Films as Art Category, American Film Festival, New York, 1960-61

1959 **Serenal** Special Mention, Bergamo, Italy, 1959-60; Special Mention, Spanish, American and Philippines Film Festival, Bilbao, 1959-60; Special Mention, International Film Festival, San Sebastian, Spain, 1959-60

1960 **Lines Vertical/Lignes verticales** and **Lines Horizontal/Lignes horizontales** Diploma of Merit, Edinburgh Film Festival, 1960-61; Outstanding Film of Year, London Film Festival, England, 1960-61; First Prize, International

Committee of Film Education and Culture, Valencia, Spain, 1960-61; First Prize, Experimental Category, International Exhibition of Cinematographic Art, Venice, 1960-61; Award of Merit, Canadian Film Awards, Toronto, 1961-62; Special Award, Vancouver Film Festival, Vancouver, B.C., 1961-62

1960 **Opening Speech McLaren/Discours de bienvenue de Norman McLaren** One of the "Outstanding Films of the Year," London Film Festival, England, 1961-62

1962 **Christmas Cracker/Caprice de Noël** First Prize, Best Animated Short Award, International Film Festival, San Francisco, California, 1964; Best Experimental Film, International Children's Film Festival, Necochea, Argentina, 1965; Landers Associates Award of Merit, Review of 16mm Non-theatrical Films Los Angeles, California, 1965-66; Exceptional Merit Award, International Festival of Short Films, Philadelphia, Pennsylvania, 1968-69

1964 **Canon** Best Recreation Film, International Children's Film Festival, Necochea, Argentina, 1965; Bronze Peacock, International Film Festival, New Delhi, India, 1964-65; First Prize — Best Animation Film, "Congrès du spectacle", Montréal, Québec, 1965-66; Second Prize, International Film Festival, New Delhi, 1965-66; Diploma of Merit, Experimental Films Category, Canadian Film Awards, Toronto, 1965-66

1965 **Mosaic/Mosaïque** Certificate of Merit, Experimental Films, Vancouver International Film Festival, 1965-66; First Prize, International Festival of Short Films, Buenos Aires, Argentina, 1966-67; Special Prize, Melbourne Film Festival, Short Film Competition, Melbourne, Australia, 1966-67; Notable Film Award, Annual Calvin Workshop, New York, 1966-67; Blue Ribbon Award, American Film Festival, New York, 1966-67

1967 **Pas de deux** Special Prize for Exceptional Quality, Canadian Film Awards, Toronto, 1968-69; Diploma of Honor, International Film Festival, Locarno, Switzerland, 1968-69; Most Original Film, International Festival of Short Films, Buenos Aires, 1968-69; Special Plaque of the Jury, International Film Festival, Chicago, 1968-69; First Prize — Best Short Film, International Film Festival, Phnom Penh, Cambodia, 1968-69; Outstanding Film of the Year Award, London Film Festival, England, 1968-69; Best Animation Film, British Film Awards, England, 1968-69; Academy of Motion Picture Arts and Science (nominated), Hollywood, 1969; Grand Prix, Short Subjects, Melbourne Film Festival, 1969; Honorable Mention, International Film Review, Colombo, Ceylon, 1969; Yorkton, Saskatchewan, International Film Festival Creative Art Award, 1969; Blue Ribbon Award, American Film Festival, New York, 1970; Prix du meilleur court métrage, International Film Festival, Panama, 1970; Festival Trophy, International Film Festival, Salerno, 1970; Prix du Secrétaire d'Etat auprès du Premier Ministre chargé de la Jeunesse, des Sports et des Loisirs, Festival of Music and Dance Motion Pictures, Menton, France, 1971; Top Choice — Jury and Audience Selection, Philadelphia International Festival of Short Films, 1971

1969 **Spheres** Special Mention, Experimental Category, International Festival Of Experimental and Documentary Films, Catholic University of Cordoba, Argentina, 1970

1971 **Synchromy/Synchromie** Special Mention Journées Internationales du Cinéma d'Animation, Annecy, France, 1971; Gold Medal (1st Prize), International Week of Cinema in Color, Barcelona, Spain, 1971; Accepted for San Francisco Film Festival, 1971; Certificate of Honor, Rockville Film Festival, Rockville, Maryland, 1972

1972 **Ballet Adagio** Meritorious Participation Certificate, San Francisco International Film Festival, 1972

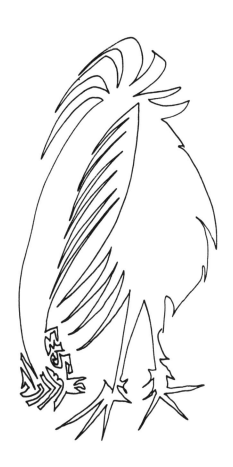

Biography

Norman McLaren is one of the world's most honored film makers. His films have won more than a hundred prizes and awards, including a Hollywood Oscar, a British Academy Award, a Grand Prize at Cannes, three first prizes at Venice, a Silver Bear at Berlin and top honors at virtually every major film festival in the world. He was named Director of the Year at the Edinburgh Film Festival, and in Chicago he won a Hugo for "the sum of his works and for his artistic and technical innovations."

McLaren was born April 11, 1914, in Stirling, Scotland, the youngest of three children. His father was a painter and interior decorator, his mother came from a farm family. He remembers seeing cartoons at the local movie theater at the age of nine, and dreaming abstract moving shapes when listening to music at the age of sixteen. At eighteen he entered the Glasgow School of Art. He specialized in interior design, but his interests turned more and more to film. In the basement of the art school, he and a fellow student found an old projector. From a local cinema they obtained old film, washed and scrubbed it clean of emulsion and used inks to make their first animated film painted directly on the celluloid.

McLaren was also interested in live action films, and in 1934 won first prize at the Scottish Amateur Film Festival with "Seven till Five" — a documentary on a day at an art school. In 1936 he and sculptor Helen Biggar made "Hell Unlimited," a strong anti-war film; it used photographs, puppets, diagrams, animation and live actors. The film took first prize at the Glasgow Film Festival.

McLaren then went to Spain as a cameraman for a film on the Civil War. "Defence of Madrid" was shown all over Britain along with "Hell Unlimited" to raise funds for the Spanish Popular Front.

John Grierson invited McLaren to join his General Post Office Film Unit, London, where he worked on documentary films and made "Love on the Wing," drawn directly on the film, in which a lively horse cavorts and metamorphosizes into wings, letters, hearts and flowers. The film was not shown publicly because the postmaster general could not accept its erotic and Freudian elements.

McLaren left the GPO and worked for a short time at the London Film Centre. Shortly before the war broke out, he moved to New York, where he painted wall murals

Biographie

Norman McLaren compte parmi les cinéastes les plus comblés d'honneurs. Ses films lui ont valu plus de cent prix et récompenses. Entre autres, un Oscar à Hollywood, une distinction de la British Academy, le Grand Prix de Cannes, trois premiers prix à Venise, l'Ours d'argent à Berlin et les honneurs les plus élevés à presque tous les festivals internationaux; le festival d'Edimbourg le nomma "Director of the Year" et, à Chicago, il mérita un Hugo pour "l'ensemble de ses travaux et pour ses innovations d'ordre artistique et technique".

McLaren est né le 11 avril 1914 à Stirling, en Écosse, le plus jeune de trois enfants. Son père était peintre et ensemblier et sa mère de famille paysanne. Il se souvient avoir vu, à l'âge de neuf ans, des dessins animés au cinéma local et avoir rêvé, à l'âge de seize ans, d'abstractions mouvantes qui lui venaient en entendant de la musique. À dix-huit ans, il entra à l'école d'art de Glasgow. Bien qu'ayant choisi la décoration intérieure comme discipline majeure, il s'intéressait de plus en plus au cinéma. En compagnie d'un autre étudiant, il découvrit un vieux projecteur au sous-sol de l'école; le cinéma local consentit à leur céder un vieux film qu'ils décapèrent et dont ils firent leur premier film d'animation, peint directement à l'encre sur la pellicule de celluloïd.

McLaren s'intéressait aussi aux films d'action. En 1934, il gagna le premier prix au festival écossais de film amateur avec un documentaire "Seven till Five", qui relatait une journée dans une école d'art. En 1936, avec le sculpteur Helen Biggar, il réalisa "Hell Unlimited", film vigoureux dirigé contre la guerre et comprenant photographies, marionnettes, diagrammes, animation et comédiens. Le film remporta le premier prix au festival de Glasgow.

McLaren alla ensuite en Espagne comme cameraman d'un film sur la guerre civile. "La Défense de Madrid", projeté partout en Grande-Bretagne, de pair avec "Hell Unlimited", servit à recueillir des fonds pour le Front populaire espagnol.

John Grierson invita McLaren à travailler à la section du film de General Post Office, à Londres. Il y réalisa des documentaires et un film "Love on the Wing" dessiné directement sur la pellicule: un cheval y cabriole puis se métamorphose en ailes, en lettres, en coeurs et en fleurs. "Le maître de poste principal" en interdit la projection publique; il ne pouvait en accepter les éléments érotiques

and made several films for the Guggenheim Museum. He drew more pictures directly onto 35 mm film, and because he was too poor to buy a sound system drew the music on as well.

In 1941, John Grierson, who was creating the National Film Board in Ottawa, asked McLaren to join him. McLaren has worked for the Film Board ever since, first in Ottawa and now in Montreal, except for two years when he was seconded to UNESCO to teach film making, first in China and then in India. His year in China inspired his Oscar-winning "Neighbours," which is his own favorite film.

Considered to be his most important films are "Blinkity Blank" which won the Palme d'or at Cannes, a Silver Bear at Berlin, a British Academy Award and top honors at film festivals in Durban, Edinburgh, London, Paris, Capetown, Montevideo, New York and Rome; "A Chairy Tale" which won a first prize at Venice and was nominated for an Oscar; "Pas de Deux" — probably the most honored of all his films, winning an Oscar nomination, top prizes in Toronto, Locarno, Buenos Aires, Chicago, Phnom Penh, London, Melbourne and Philadelphia; "Lines Vertical" and "Lines Horizontal" which took top honors in Venice, as well as in Edinburgh, Valencia, Toronto and Vancouver; and of course "Neighbours" which was honored in Toronto, Boston, Salerno, Rome and Yorkton, Saskatchewan, as well as in Hollywood.

In 1971 McLaren was presented with the Outstanding Achievement Award of Public Service of Canada, the highest honor the government can give a public servant, and in 1972 he was made a member of the Order of Canada. He has also won Canada's prestigious Molson Prize for outstanding contributions to the arts, humanities and social sciences. In the fall of 1975 he was invited to Los Angeles to receive the Anni Award of the International Animated Film Society.

et freudiens.

McLaren laissa la G.P.O. et travailla un temps à la London Film Centre. Peu de temps avant la guerre, il déménagea à New York où il devint peintre de "murales" et réalisateur de films pour le compte du musée Guggenheim. Il fit d'autres films en dessinant directement sur de la pellicule de 35 mm; trop désargenté pour acquérir un appareil de sonorisation, il y dessinait également la musique.

En 1941, John Grierson mit sur pied l'Office national du film. Il y invita McLaren qui y est resté depuis, à Ottawa tout d'abord, à Montréal par la suite. Il faut faire exception de deux années où, pour le compte de l'Unesco, il enseigna la technique de fabrication du film en Chine puis en Inde. Son séjour en Chine lui inspira "Les Voisins", qui lui valut un Oscar, et qui est encore son film préféré.

Voyons les titres que l'on considère les plus importants. "Blinkity Blank" valut au cinéaste la Palme d'or à Cannes, l'Ours d'argent à Berlin, une distinction de la British Academy et les honneurs les plus élevés aux festivals du film de Durban, Edimbourg, Londres, Paris, Capetown, Montevideo, New York et Rome. "Il était une chaise" lui obtint un premier prix à Venise et la mise en candidature pour un Oscar. "Pas de deux" est probablement le film le plus couvert d'honneurs: mise en candidature pour un Oscar, les plus hauts prix à Toronto, Locarno, Buenos Aires, Chicago, Phnom Penh, Londres, Melbourne et Philadelphie. "Lignes verticales" et "Lignes horizontales" remportèrent les plus grands honneurs aussi bien à Venise qu'à Edimbourg, Valencia, Toronto et Vancouver. Et, bien sûr, "Les Voisins" méritèrent les honneurs à Toronto, Boston, Salerno, Rome, Yorkton (Saskatchewan) tout autant qu'à Hollywood.

En 1971, McLaren obtint le plus grand honneur que l'État puisse décerner à un fonctionnaire: la distinction accordée en raison d'éminents services rendus à la fonction publique (The Outstanding Achievement Award of Public Service of Canada) et, en 1972, il fut reçu "member of the Order of Canada". Il obtint également le prestigieux prix Molson pour sa contribution exceptionnelle dans le domaine des arts, de l'humanisme et des sciences sociales. À l'automne de 1975, il fut invité à Los Angeles pour recevoir le Anni Award de la Société internationale du film d'animation.

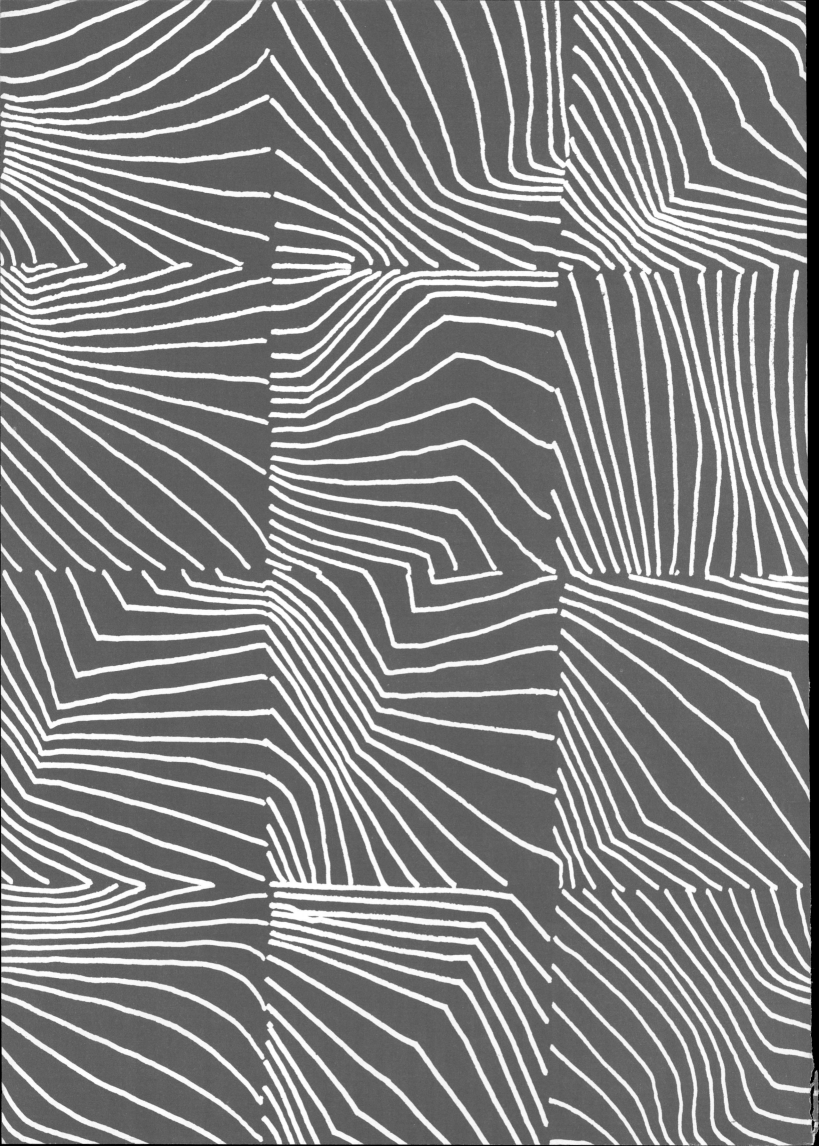